Betty Crocker's
CHRISTMAS
COOKBOOK

GOLDEN PRESS / NEW YORK

Western Publishing Company, Inc.
Racine, Wisconsin

Director of Photography: Len Weiss

Illustrator: Ray Skibinski

First Printing, 1982

Printed in the U.S.A. by Western Publishing Company, Inc.
Published by Golden Press, New York, New York.
Library of Congress Catalog Card Number: 82-80289

Golden® and Golden Press® are trademarks of Western Publishing Company, Inc.
ISBN 0-307-09820-6

Contents

Foreword

Christmas, like no other time of the year, evokes our most cherished—and delicious—memories: tempting cranberry pies, cooling on the back porch . . . the first buttery bite of Grandmother's stollen . . . the crackle of roasting chestnuts . . . fragrant fruitcakes and rum balls and gingerbread men. The challenge is to translate those remembrances of Christmases past into the era of Christmas present—and in so doing, perhaps create some brand-new memories. And *Betty Crocker's Christmas Cookbook* will help you do just that. We've included only our best Christmas recipes, those that will adapt to a variety of needs and occasions. And they've been thoroughly tested, so you can be sure they'll succeed.

To begin with, you'll find a host of recipes for cookies and candies, for delectable desserts and for holiday breads of all shapes, sizes and flavors. For Christmas Day dinner, you can choose from traditional favorites, with all their trimmings, as well as change-of-pace feasts. But not forgetting that this is the season for entertaining, there are menus for every kind of holiday get-together: from elegant buffets and special suppers to brunches, open houses and casual "at homes."

'Tis the season of sharing, too, and what more thoughtful way to say "Merry Christmas" than with a gaily-wrapped gift from your own kitchen. Included are more than a score of our favorites: jams and jellies, spreads and sauces, special sweets—with ideas for wrapping them as well. Included, too, are enchanting salt dough ornaments and decorations (heirlooms for tomorrow) plus step-by-step directions for making your own gingerbread centerpieces—a charming chalet and Santa's sleigh, complete with eager-to-fly reindeer.

Whatever your plans for celebrating the holidays, we're confident that this book will provide all the help you need to make the joys of the season—the good food, the good fellowship—thrive in your home. It's our merry Christmas present to you.

Betty Crocker

Opposite: Saint Lucia Crown (page 75)

Traditions from the Christmas Kitchen

Cookies, Candies and Sweet Snacks

What's as traditional as mistletoe over the door? Overflowing cookie jars and plates heaped high with homemade sweets. Here is a nostalgic sampling of old (and old-world) Christmas favorites as well as contemporary, easy-to-fix treats. Many are packable, perfect for mailing to far-flung friends (as well as sharing with the postman). Littlest holiday helpers will be eager to decorate the cookie cutouts for both the table and the tree. And the handy, make-it-yourself cookie mix not only starts off half a dozen delectables, it's a thoughtful gift in itself. Or fill up a pretty glass or a colorful tin with your own irresistible candies and snacks: They will spread good tidings in the best of taste.

Stained Glass Cookie

Deluxe Sugar Cookies

1½ cups powdered sugar
 1 cup margarine or butter, softened
 1 egg
 1 teaspoon vanilla
 ½ teaspoon almond extract
2½ cups all-purpose flour
 1 teaspoon baking soda
 1 teaspoon cream of tartar

Mix powdered sugar, margarine, egg, vanilla and almond extract. Stir in flour, baking soda and cream of tartar. Cover and refrigerate at least 3 hours.

Heat oven to 375°. Divide dough into halves. Roll each half ³⁄₁₆ inch thick on lightly floured cloth-covered board. Cut into desired shapes with cookie cutters. Place on ungreased cookie sheet. Bake until edges are light brown, 7 to 8 minutes. Frost and decorate as desired.   *About 5 dozen 2-inch cookies.*

Stained Glass Cookies: Before refrigerating, divide dough into halves. Divide 1 half into 3 to 5 parts. Tint each part with a different food color. Wrap each part and the plain dough separately in plastic wrap and refrigerate at least 3 hours. Roll plain dough ⅛ inch thick on lightly floured cloth-covered board. Cut with bell, star, tree and other decorative cookie cutters. Place on ungreased cookie sheet. Roll tinted doughs ⅛ inch thick; cut out different shapes to fit on each cookie. Heat oven to 375°. Bake until golden, 7 to 8 minutes.

Merry Christmas Molasses Cookies

⅔ cup packed brown sugar	4 teaspoons ground
⅔ cup shortening	cinnamon
1⅓ cups molasses	2 teaspoons ground ginger
2 eggs	2 teaspoons baking soda
5½ cups all-purpose flour	1 teaspoon salt

Mix brown sugar, shortening and molasses. Stir in remaining ingredients. Cover and refrigerate at least 1 hour.

Heat oven to 375°. Roll dough ¼ inch thick on lightly floured cloth-covered board. Cut into desired shapes with cookie cutters. Place about 1 inch apart on lightly greased cookie sheet. Bake until no indentation remains when touched, 7 to 8 minutes; cool. Frost and decorate as desired.   *About 5 dozen 3-inch cookies.*

Note: For crisper cookies, roll dough ⅛ inch thick; bake 6 to 7 minutes.

Holiday Cutouts

Prepare dough as directed for Deluxe Sugar Cookies (page 6), Merry Christmas Molasses Cookies (above) or Light Ginger Cookies (page 10). After rolling out dough, cut into assorted shapes with cookie cutters or cut around patterns traced from storybook illustrations. If desired, cut small appliqués of dough and press on cookies (see cat cookie, page 8). Cookies can be decorated before baking with Baked-On Decorators' Frosting or afterwards with Creamy Decorators' Frosting (below). Use colored sugars, sprinkles and nonpareils — and your imagination! (See pages 8 and 9 for some ideas.)

To outline designs on baked cookies, place frosting in a decorators' tube. Or cut off a tiny corner of a #10 envelope or small strong plastic bag. Fill with about ⅓ cup frosting at a time. Convenient ready-to-use frosting tubes can also be used.

To hang cookies on a Christmas tree or wreath, loop a piece of string and press ends into underside of each cookie before baking or use a drinking straw to poke a hole.

BAKED-ON DECORATORS' FROSTING

Mix ⅓ cup all-purpose flour and ⅓ cup margarine or butter, softened, until smooth. Stir in 1½ teaspoons hot water and, if desired, 2 or 3 drops food color. Place in decorators' tube with #3 writing tip. Outline, write or make designs on unbaked rolled cookies. Bake cookies as directed in recipe.   *Enough for 2 to 3 dozen cookies.*

CREAMY DECORATORS' FROSTING

Beat 1 cup powdered sugar, ½ teaspoon vanilla and about 1 tablespoon water or 1 to 2 tablespoons half-and-half until smooth and of spreading consistency. Tint with food color if desired.   *Enough for 3 to 5 dozen cookies.*

Baked-On Decorators' Frosting transforms Merry Christmas Molasses Cookies into snowflakes

Overleaf: A colorful assortment of Holiday Cutouts

Light Ginger Cookies

1 cup powdered sugar
1 cup margarine or butter, softened
1 tablespoon vinegar
2¼ cups all-purpose flour

1½ to 2 teaspoons ground ginger
¾ teaspoon baking soda
¼ teaspoon salt

Heat oven to 400°. Mix powdered sugar, margarine and vinegar. Stir in remaining ingredients. (If dough is too dry, work in milk or cream, 1 teaspoon at a time.)

Roll dough ⅛ inch thick on lightly floured cloth-covered board. Cut into desired shapes with cookie cutters. Place on ungreased cookie sheet. Bake until light brown, 6 to 8 minutes. Cool slightly; carefully remove from cookie sheet. Decorate with Creamy Decorators' Frosting (page 7) if desired.   *About 4 dozen 3-inch cookies.*

Christmas Pinwheels

1 cup sugar
¾ cup shortening (part margarine or butter, softened)
2 eggs
1 teaspoon vanilla

2½ cups all-purpose flour
1 teaspoon baking powder
1 teaspoon salt
About ⅓ cup raspberry jam

Mix sugar, shortening, eggs and vanilla. Stir in flour, baking powder and salt. Cover and refrigerate at least 1 hour.

Roll about ⅓ of the dough at a time into 10-inch square on lightly floured cloth-covered board. Cut into 2½-inch squares. Cut squares diagonally from each corner almost to center (see diagram). Place about ½ teaspoon jam on center of each square. Fold every other point to center to make a pinwheel. Heat oven to 400°. Place pinwheels on ungreased cookie sheet. Bake until light brown, about 6 minutes.   *About 4 dozen cookies.*

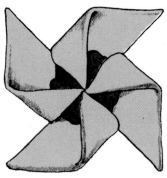

Christmas Pinwheels

Snowflake Cookies: After refrigerating, roll dough ⅛ inch thick on lightly floured cloth-covered board. Cut into 1½- to 2-inch star shapes. Place on ungreased cookie sheet. Brush half of the cookies with milk, then sprinkle with granulated sugar. Bake until light brown, 6 to 8 minutes. Mix ½ cup powdered sugar and 1½ to 2 teaspoons water. Put cookies together in pairs with about ¼ teaspoon powdered sugar mixture. Place sugared cookies on top, alternating points of stars (see diagram).   *About 2½ dozen cookies.*

Snowflake Cookies

Cinnamon Stars

1 cup sugar
¾ cup shortening (part
    margarine or butter,
    softened)
1 egg
1 egg, separated
2 teaspoons lemon juice

2⅓ cups all-purpose flour
2 teaspoons ground
    cinnamon
1 teaspoon baking powder
1 teaspoon salt
½ cup finely chopped nuts

Mix sugar, shortening, whole egg, the egg yolk and lemon juice. Stir in remaining ingredients except egg white. Cover and refrigerate at least 1 hour.

Heat oven to 400°. Roll dough ⅛ inch thick on lightly floured cloth-covered board. Cut into star shapes. Place on ungreased cookie sheet. Beat egg white until foamy; brush on cookies. Bake until light brown, 6 to 8 minutes.   *About 6 dozen 2½-inch cookies.*

Zimtsterne, or Cinnamon Stars, are popular holiday cookies in Germany and Switzerland; this is an easy adaptation.

Lebkuchen

½ cup honey
½ cup molasses
¾ cup packed brown sugar
1 egg
1 teaspoon grated lemon
    peel
1 tablespoon lemon juice
2¾ cups all-purpose flour
1 teaspoon ground allspice

1 teaspoon ground
    cinnamon
1 teaspoon ground cloves
1 teaspoon ground nutmeg
½ teaspoon baking soda
⅓ cup cut-up citron
⅓ cup chopped nuts
    Cookie Glaze (below)

Mix honey and molasses in saucepan. Heat to boiling; remove from heat. Cool completely. Stir in brown sugar, egg, lemon peel and lemon juice. Stir in remaining ingredients except Cookie Glaze. Cover and refrigerate at least 8 hours.

Heat oven to 400°. Roll about ¼ of the dough at a time ¼ inch thick on lightly floured cloth-covered board (keep remaining dough refrigerated). Cut into rectangles, 2½x1½ inches. Place about 1 inch apart on greased cookie sheet. Bake until no indentation remains when touched, 10 to 12 minutes. Brush glaze over cookies. Immediately remove from cookie sheet.   *About 5 dozen cookies.*

COOKIE GLAZE
Mix 1 cup sugar and ½ cup water in saucepan. Cook over medium heat to 230° or just until small amount of mixture spins a 2-inch thread; remove from heat. Stir in ¼ cup powdered sugar. (If glaze becomes sugary while brushing cookies, heat slightly, adding a little water, until clear again.)

Note: Store cookies in airtight container. For softer cookies, store with a slice of apple or orange in airtight container; replace fruit frequently.

Spice-scented Lebkuchen have been a Christmas tradition in German homes for many centuries.

Magic Window Cookies

1 cup sugar
¾ cup shortening (part margarine or butter, softened)
2 eggs
1 teaspoon vanilla or ½ teaspoon lemon extract

2½ cups all-purpose flour
1 teaspoon baking powder
1 teaspoon salt
About 5 rolls (about .79 ounce each) ring-shaped hard candy

Mix sugar, shortening, eggs and vanilla. Stir in flour, baking powder and salt. Cover and refrigerate at least 1 hour.

Roll dough ⅛ inch thick on lightly floured cloth-covered board. Cut into desired shapes with cookie cutters. Place cookies on aluminum foil-covered cookie sheet. Cut out designs from cookies using smaller cutters or your own patterns. Place whole or partially crushed candy in cutouts, depending on size and shape of design. (To crush candy, place between paper towels and tap lightly. As candy melts easily, leave pieces as large as possible.) If cookies are to be hung, make a hole in each ¼ inch from top with end of plastic straw.

Heat oven to 375°. Bake until cookies are very light brown and candy is melted, 7 to 9 minutes. If candy has not filled out cutout design, immediately spread with metal spatula. Cool completely on cookie sheet. Gently remove cookies.   *About 6 dozen 3-inch cookies.*

Paintbrush Cookies

1 cup sugar
¾ cup shortening (part margarine or butter, softened)
2 eggs

1 teaspoon vanilla
2½ cups all-purpose flour
1 teaspoon baking powder
1 teaspoon salt
Egg Yolk Paint (below)

Mix sugar, shortening, eggs and vanilla. Stir in flour, baking powder and salt. Cover and refrigerate at least 1 hour.

Roll dough ⅛ inch thick on lightly floured cloth-covered board. Cut into desired shapes with cookie cutters. Place on ungreased cookie sheet. Prepare Egg Yolk Paint. Paint designs on cookies with small paintbrushes. Heat oven to 400°. Bake until cookies are delicate golden brown, 6 to 8 minutes.   *About 4 dozen 3-inch cookies.*

EGG YOLK PAINT
Mix 1 egg yolk and ¼ teaspoon water. Divide mixture among several small custard cups. Tint each with different food color to make bright colors. If paint thickens while standing, stir in few drops water.

Magic Window Cookies, pretty enough to hang on the tree

Opposite: Paintbrush Cookies are special fun at children's holiday parties

Peppernuts

¾ cup packed brown sugar
½ cup shortening
½ cup molasses
1 egg
1 tablespoon hot water
3 drops anise oil
3⅓ cups all-purpose flour

½ teaspoon baking soda
½ teaspoon ground
cinnamon
½ teaspoon ground cloves
¼ teaspoon salt
⅛ teaspoon white pepper

Mix brown sugar, shortening, molasses, egg, water and anise oil. Stir in remaining ingredients. Knead dough until right consistency for molding. Heat oven to 350°. Shape dough into ¾-inch balls. Place about 1 inch apart on ungreased cookie sheet. Bake until bottoms are golden brown, about 12 minutes. *About 8 dozen cookies.*

Note: For the traditionally hard Peppernut, store in airtight container. For softer cookies, store with a slice of apple in airtight container; replace apple frequently.

Almond Cookie Wreaths

1 cup sugar
1 cup margarine or butter,
softened
½ cup milk
1 egg
1 teaspoon vanilla

1 teaspoon almond extract
3½ cups all-purpose flour
1 teaspoon baking powder
¼ teaspoon salt
½ teaspoon green food color
Red candied cherries

Mix sugar, margarine, milk, egg, vanilla and almond extract. Stir in flour, baking powder and salt. Divide dough into halves. Tint 1 half with food color. (For monochromatic wreath, tint second half with 3 drops green food color.) Cover and refrigerate at least 4 hours.

For each wreath, shape 1 teaspoon dough from each half into 4-inch rope. For smooth, even ropes, roll back and forth on sugared surface. Place 1 green and 1 white rope side by side; press together lightly and twist. Place on ungreased cookie sheet. Shape each into circle with ends meeting; press bits of candied cherries on wreath for holly berries. Heat oven to 375°. Bake until set and very light brown, 9 to 12 minutes. *About 4½ dozen cookies.*

Chocolate-Nut Fingers: For each cookie, roll 1 teaspoon dough into 2½-inch length. Heat ½ cup semisweet chocolate chips until melted. After baking, dip ends of cookies into melted chocolate, then into chopped nuts. *About 8 dozen cookies.*

Peppermint Candy Canes: Substitute 1 teaspoon peppermint extract for the almond extract. Substitute ½ teaspoon red food color for the green. Roll ropes on floured surface. After placing on cookie sheet, curve down top of cookie to form handle of cane. After baking, immediately sprinkle cookies with mixture of 2 tablespoons crushed peppermint candy and 2 tablespoons sugar.

Almond Cookie Wreaths,
Peppermint Candy Canes and
Chocolate-Nut Fingers

Berlinerkranzer

1 cup sugar	2 eggs
¾ cup margarine or butter, softened	4 cups all-purpose flour
	1 egg white
¾ cup shortening	2 tablespoons sugar
2 teaspoons grated orange peel	Red candied cherries
	Green candied citron

"Berlin Wreaths" are popular Christmas cookies in Norway, where this recipe originated.

Mix 1 cup sugar, the margarine, shortening, orange peel and whole eggs. Stir in flour. Shape dough by rounded teaspoonfuls into ropes, about 6 inches long and ¼ inch in diameter. Form each rope into circle, crossing ends and tucking under. (This shaping method is easier than the traditional method of tying knots.) Place on ungreased cookie sheet.

Heat oven to 400°. Beat egg white and 2 tablespoons sugar until foamy; brush over tops of cookies. For holly berries, press bits of red candied cherries on center of knot; add little jagged leaves cut from citron. Bake until set but not brown, 10 to 12 minutes. Immediately remove from cookie sheet.   *About 6 dozen cookies.*

Chocolate-Peppermint Pretzels

1 cup powdered sugar	2½ cups all-purpose flour
½ cup margarine or butter, softened	½ cup cocoa
	1 teaspoon salt
½ cup shortening	Chocolate Glaze (below)
1 egg	¼ cup crushed peppermint candy
1½ teaspoons vanilla	

Mix powdered sugar, margarine, shortening, egg and vanilla. Stir in flour, cocoa and salt. Knead level tablespoonful of dough with hands until right consistency for molding. Roll into pencil-like rope, about 9 inches long, on board. Twist into pretzel shape on ungreased cookie sheet (see diagram). Repeat with remaining dough.

Heat oven to 375°. Bake until set, about 9 minutes. Let stand 1 to 2 minutes before removing from cookie sheet; cool. Dip tops of pretzels into Chocolate Glaze. Sprinkle with peppermint candy.   *About 4 dozen cookies.*

CHOCOLATE GLAZE
Heat 2 squares (1 ounce each) unsweetened chocolate and 2 tablespoons margarine or butter over low heat until melted; remove from heat. Beat in 2 cups powdered sugar and 3 to 4 tablespoons water until smooth and of desired consistency.

Chocolate-Peppermint Pretzels

Sugarplum Cookies

¾ cup sugar
½ cup margarine or butter, softened
½ cup shortening
1 egg
2½ cups all-purpose flour
1½ teaspoons vanilla
½ teaspoon baking powder
⅛ teaspoon salt
¾ cup cut-up dried or candied fruit or 2 to 3 ounces filberts
Creamy Frosting (below)

Mix sugar, margarine, shortening and egg. Stir in flour, vanilla, baking powder and salt. Heat oven to 375°. Shape dough by teaspoonfuls around fruit to form balls. Place about 1 inch apart on ungreased cookie sheet. Bake until delicate brown, 12 to 15 minutes; cool. Spread tops of cookies with Creamy Frosting. Decorate with colored sugar, nonpareils or chopped nuts if desired. *About 7 dozen cookies.*

CREAMY FROSTING
Mix 1½ cups powdered sugar, ½ teaspoon vanilla and 2 to 3 tablespoons water until of desired consistency.

Turtle Cookies

½ cup packed brown sugar
½ cup margarine or butter, softened
2 tablespoons water
1 teaspoon vanilla
1½ cups all-purpose flour
⅛ teaspoon salt
Pecan halves
8 caramels, each cut into fourths
Chocolate Glaze (below)

Mix brown sugar, margarine, water and vanilla. Stir in flour and salt until dough holds together. (If dough is dry, stir in 1 to 2 teaspoons water.)

Heat oven to 350°. For each cookie, group 3 to 5 pecan halves, split if necessary, on ungreased cookie sheet. Shape dough by teaspoonfuls around caramel pieces; press firmly onto center of each group of nuts. Bake until set but not brown, 12 to 15 minutes; cool. Dip tops of cookies into Chocolate Glaze. *About 2½ dozen cookies.*

CHOCOLATE GLAZE
Beat 1 cup powdered sugar, 1 tablespoon water, 1 ounce melted unsweetened chocolate (cool) and 1 teaspoon vanilla until smooth. If necessary, stir in water, 1 teaspoon at a time, until frosting is of desired consistency.

Santa Claus Cookies

1 cup granulated sugar	½ teaspoon salt
½ cup shortening	Creamy Frosting (page 16)
2 tablespoons milk	Miniature marshmallows
1 teaspoon grated lemon peel	Red sugar
1 egg	Currants or semisweet
2 cups all-purpose flour	chocolate chips
1 teaspoon baking powder	Red cinnamon candies
½ teaspoon baking soda	Shredded coconut

Mix granulated sugar, shortening, milk, lemon peel and egg. Stir in flour, baking powder, baking soda and salt. Heat oven to 400°. Shape dough into 1¼-inch balls. Place about 2 inches apart on ungreased cookie sheet; flatten each to about 2½-inch diameter with greased bottom of glass dipped in sugar. Bake until edges are light brown, 8 to 10 minutes; cool.

Spread cookie with small amount of Creamy Frosting. Press on miniature marshmallow for tassel of cap. Sprinkle top third of cookie with red sugar. Press 2 currants for eyes and red cinnamon candy for nose into center third. Sprinkle bottom third with coconut for beard. Frost and decorate each cookie before starting another. *About 1½ dozen cookies.*

Santa Claus Cookie Pops: After shaping dough into balls, insert wooden ice-cream sticks halfway into balls; continue as directed.

Chocolate-Almond Teacakes

¾ cup margarine or butter,
   softened
⅓ cup powdered sugar
1 cup all-purpose flour

½ cup instant cocoa mix
½ cup toasted diced almonds
   Powdered sugar

Mix margarine and ⅓ cup powdered sugar. Stir in flour, cocoa mix and almonds. (If dough is soft, cover and refrigerate until firm enough to shape.) Heat oven to 325°. Shape dough into 1-inch balls. Place about 2 inches apart on ungreased cookie sheet. Bake until set, about 20 minutes. Dip tops into powdered sugar while warm; cool. Dip into powdered sugar again.   *About 4 dozen cookies.*

Coconut-Pecan Balls

1 cup margarine or butter,
   softened
½ cup sugar
2 teaspoons vanilla
2 cups all-purpose flour

¼ teaspoon salt
4 dozen pecan halves
1 egg white
1 tablespoon water
1½ cups flaked coconut

Mix margarine, sugar and vanilla. Stir in flour and salt. (If dough is soft, cover and refrigerate until firm enough to shape.) Heat oven to 350°. Shape dough around pecan halves to form 1-inch balls. Beat egg white and water with fork. Dip balls into egg white mixture; roll in coconut. Place about 1 inch apart on ungreased cookie sheet. Bake until light brown, 14 to 15 minutes. Store in tightly covered container.   *About 4 dozen cookies.*

Candied Fruit Cookies

1 cup powdered sugar
1 cup margarine or butter,
   softened
1 egg
2¼ cups all-purpose flour

¼ teaspoon cream of tartar
1 cup whole candied cherries
½ cup cut-up mixed candied
   fruit
½ cup chopped pecans

Mix powdered sugar, margarine and egg. Stir in remaining ingredients. Divide dough into halves. Shape each half into roll, 1½ inches in diameter. Wrap and refrigerate at least 4 hours.

Heat oven to 375°. Cut rolls into ⅛-inch slices. Place 1 inch apart on ungreased cookie sheet. Bake until set, about 8 minutes. Immediately remove from cookie sheet.   *About 6 dozen cookies.*

Lemon Cookie Sandwiches

½ cup sugar	1½ cups all-purpose flour
½ cup margarine or butter, softened	½ teaspoon salt
	¼ teaspoon baking soda
2 eggs, separated	⅔ cup finely chopped nuts
1 tablespoon water	Lemon Filling (below)
1 teaspoon vanilla	

Mix sugar, margarine, egg yolks, water and vanilla. Stir in flour, salt and baking soda. Divide dough into halves. Shape each half into roll, 7x1½ inches. Wrap and refrigerate at least 4 hours.

Heat oven to 400°. Cut rolls into ⅛-inch slices. Place 1 inch apart on ungreased cookie sheet. Beat egg whites slightly; stir in nuts. Spoon ½ teaspoon nut mixture onto half of the slices, leaving remaining slices plain. Bake until edges begin to brown, about 6 minutes. Immediately remove from cookie sheet; cool. Put cookies together in pairs with Lemon Filling, placing nut-topped cookies on top. *About 4 dozen cookies.*

LEMON FILLING
Beat 1 cup powdered sugar, 2 teaspoons margarine or butter, softened, 1 teaspoon grated lemon peel and 1½ tablespoons lemon juice until smooth.

Christmas Bells

½ cup sugar	1 teaspoon vanilla
¼ cup margarine or butter, softened	1½ cups all-purpose flour
	½ teaspoon salt
¼ cup shortening	¼ teaspoon baking soda
1 egg	Red or green food color

Mix sugar, margarine, shortening, egg and vanilla. Stir in flour, salt and baking soda. Stir food color into ⅔ of the dough. Shape into roll, 10x1½ inches. Form bell shape by pressing top of roll together and leaving lower half flared and curved (see photograph). Wrap and refrigerate at least 1 hour.

Reserve ¼ cup of the plain dough for clappers. Roll remaining plain dough into rectangle, about 10x5 inches, on waxed paper. Wrap around bell-shaped roll. Wrap and refrigerate at least 8 hours.

Heat oven to 375°. Cut roll into ⅛-inch slices. Place on ungreased cookie sheet. Place tiny ball of reserved dough at bottom of each bell for clapper. Bake until edges are light brown, 7 to 8 minutes. *About 4½ dozen cookies.*

Christmas Balls: Do not shape dough roll into bell. After wrapping with plain dough, roll in colored shot.

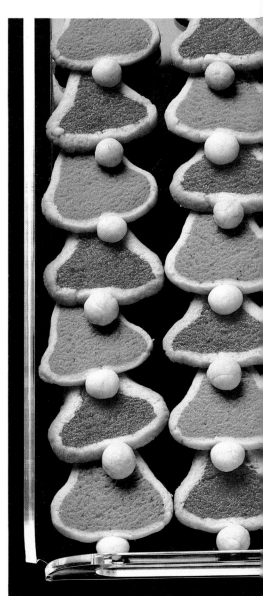

Christmas Bells

Christmas Cookie Slices

1 cup sugar	1½ teaspoons vanilla
1 cup margarine or butter, softened	3 cups all-purpose flour
	1 teaspoon salt
2 eggs	½ teaspoon baking soda

Mix sugar, margarine, eggs and vanilla. Stir in remaining ingredients. Divide into 3 equal parts. Shape each part into roll, about 1½ inches in diameter. Wrap and refrigerate at least 4 hours.

Heat oven to 400°. Cut rolls into ⅛-inch slices. Place about 1 inch apart on ungreased cookie sheet. Bake 8 to 10 minutes. Immediately remove from cookie sheet.   *About 7 dozen cookies.*

Butterscotch Slices: Substitute packed brown sugar for the granulated sugar.

Christmas Trees: Shape roll into triangle; coat sides with green sugar. Continue as directed. Cut tree trunks from several slices; attach trunks to trees on cookie sheet, overlapping slightly.

Cookie Tarts: Cut out centers of half of the unbaked cookies with ¾-inch cutters, or design your own patterns. Spoon ½ teaspoon red jelly or jam onto uncut slices; top with cutout slices. Press edges to seal.

Holiday Sugar Slices: Coat rolls with red or green sugar or multicolored candies.

Nutmeg Slices: Add ½ teaspoon ground nutmeg with the flour. Coat rolls with mixture of ¼ cup sugar and ½ teaspoon ground nutmeg.

Nutty Slices: Coat rolls with chopped nuts.

Orange-Almond Slices: Mix in 1 tablespoon grated orange peel with the margarine and ½ cup cut-up blanched almonds with the flour.

Peppermint Pinwheels: Decrease vanilla to 1 teaspoon; add 1 teaspoon peppermint extract. After dough is mixed, divide into halves. Stir ½ teaspoon red or green food color into 1 half. Cover both halves and refrigerate 1 hour. Roll plain dough into rectangle, about 16x9 inches, on lightly floured surface. Repeat with colored dough; place on plain dough. Roll doughs together about ¼ inch thick. Roll up tightly, beginning at 16-inch side. Wrap and refrigerate. Continue as directed.   *About 7 dozen cookies.*

Ribbon Bar Cookies: Decrease vanilla to 1 teaspoon; add 1 teaspoon peppermint extract. After dough is mixed, divide into halves. Stir ½ teaspoon red or green food color into 1 half. Cover both halves and refrigerate 1 hour. Shape each half into 2 strips, each about 9x2½ inches, on very lightly floured surface. Layer strips, alternating colors; press together. Wrap and refrigerate. Continue as directed.   *About 5½ dozen cookies.*

Opposite: A rainbow of Christmas cookies, all from this basic recipe. Top to bottom: Peppermint Pinwheels, Christmas Trees, Ribbon Bar Cookies, Holiday Sugar Slices and Cookie Tarts

Like biting into a little fruitcake....

Christmas Jewels

½ cup molasses
⅓ cup shortening
¼ cup sugar
1 egg
1½ cups all-purpose flour
1 teaspoon ground
   cinnamon
1 teaspoon ground mace
1 teaspoon ground nutmeg
½ teaspoon baking soda
¼ teaspoon salt
¼ teaspoon ground allspice
¼ teaspoon ground ginger
2½ cups mixed candied fruit
   (about 16 ounces)
2 cups coarsely chopped
   nuts

Heat oven to 325°. Mix molasses, shortening, sugar and egg. Stir in remaining ingredients. Drop by teaspoonfuls about 1 inch apart onto lightly greased cookie sheet. Bake 12 to 15 minutes. *About 6 dozen cookies.*

Gumdrop Cookies

2 cups packed brown sugar
1 cup shortening
½ cup buttermilk or water
2 eggs
3½ cups all-purpose flour
1 teaspoon baking soda
1 teaspoon salt
3 to 4 cups cut-up gumdrops

Mix brown sugar, shortening, buttermilk and eggs. Stir in flour, baking soda, salt and gumdrops. Cover and refrigerate at least 1 hour.

Heat oven to 400°. Drop dough by rounded teaspoonfuls about 2 inches apart onto ungreased cookie sheet. Bake until almost no indentation remains when touched, 8 to 10 minutes. Immediately remove from cookie sheet. *About 6 dozen cookies.*

Note: Scissors, dipped occasionally into hot water, cut gumdrops easily.

Fruit Ginger Drops

1 package (14.5 ounces)
   gingerbread mix
½ cup water
1 cup cut-up candied fruit
½ cup chopped nuts

Heat oven to 375°. Mix gingerbread mix and water. Stir in candied fruit and nuts. Drop by teaspoonfuls onto lightly greased cookie sheet. Bake 10 to 12 minutes. *About 3 dozen cookies.*

Gumdrop Ginger Drops: Substitute ⅔ cup cut-up gumdrops for the candied fruit.

Mincemeat Ginger Drops: Substitute 1 cup prepared mincemeat for the candied fruit.

Raisin Ginger Drops: Substitute 1 cup raisins for the candied fruit.

Cherry-Coconut Macaroons

3 egg whites
¼ teaspoon cream of tartar
⅛ teaspoon salt
¾ cup sugar
¼ teaspoon almond extract

Red or green food color
2 cups flaked coconut
12 candied cherries, each cut
   into fourths

Beat egg whites, cream of tartar and salt in small mixer bowl until foamy. Beat in sugar, 1 tablespoon at a time; continue beating until stiff and glossy. Do not underbeat. Transfer to large bowl. Fold in almond extract, 3 drops food color and the coconut.

Heat oven to 300°. Drop mixture by teaspoonfuls about 1 inch apart onto aluminum foil-covered cookie sheet. Place a cherry piece on each cookie. Bake just until edges are light brown, 20 to 25 minutes. Cool 10 minutes; remove from foil. Store in airtight container no longer than 2 weeks or freeze no longer than 1 month. *3½ to 4 dozen cookies.*

Mint Macaroons: Substitute ¼ teaspoon peppermint extract for the almond extract. After beating, fold in 1 package (6 ounces) semi-sweet chocolate chips, reserving 3½ to 4 dozen chocolate chips. Substitute reserved chips for the cherry pieces.

Cranberry Cookies

1 cup granulated sugar
¾ cup packed brown sugar
½ cup margarine or butter,
   softened
¼ cup milk
2 tablespoons orange juice
1 egg
3 cups all-purpose flour

1 teaspoon baking powder
½ teaspoon salt
¼ teaspoon baking soda
2½ cups coarsely chopped
   cranberries
1 cup chopped nuts
   Browned Butter Glaze
   (below), if desired

Heat oven to 375°. Mix sugars and margarine. Stir in milk, orange juice and egg. Stir in remaining ingredients except Browned Butter Glaze. Drop by rounded teaspoonfuls about 2 inches apart onto greased cookie sheet. Bake until light brown, 10 to 15 minutes. Cool; spread with glaze. *About 5½ dozen cookies.*

BROWNED BUTTER GLAZE
Heat ⅓ cup margarine or butter over low heat until golden brown; cool slightly. Stir in 2 cups powdered sugar and 1½ teaspoons vanilla. Beat in 2 to 4 tablespoons hot water until smooth and of desired consistency.

Mincemeat Bars

½ cup margarine or butter, softened
¼ cup shortening
1 cup packed brown sugar
1½ cups all-purpose flour
1 teaspoon salt

½ teaspoon baking soda
1 cup quick-cooking oats
1 jar (28 ounces) prepared mincemeat
½ cup chopped walnuts or almonds

Heat oven to 400°. Mix margarine, shortening and brown sugar. Stir in flour, salt, baking soda and oats. Press half of the crumbly mixture in greased baking pan, 13x9x2 inches. Mix mincemeat and walnuts; spread over top. Sprinkle with remaining crumbly mixture; press lightly.

Bake until light brown, 25 to 30 minutes. While warm, make a diagonal cut from corner to corner. Continue cutting parallel to first cut, each about 1½ inches apart. Repeat, cutting diagonally in opposite direction. *About 3½ dozen bars.*

Date-Apricot Bars: Mix 1¼ cups cut-up dates, 1½ cups cut-up dried apricots, ½ cup sugar and 1½ cups water in saucepan. Cook over medium-low heat, stirring constantly, until thickened, about 10 minutes. Substitute date-apricot filling for the mincemeat filling.

Date-Raisin Bars: Mix 1½ cups cut-up dates, 1½ cups raisins, ¼ cup sugar and 1½ cups water in saucepan. Cook over low heat, stirring constantly, until thickened, about 10 minutes. Substitute date-raisin filling for the mincemeat filling.

Raspberry Jam Strips

1 cup margarine or butter, softened
½ cup granulated sugar
½ cup packed brown sugar
1 egg

1 teaspoon vanilla
2½ cups all-purpose flour
1 teaspoon baking powder
½ cup raspberry jam
Almond Glaze (below)

Mix margarine, sugars, egg and vanilla. Stir in flour and baking powder. (If dough is soft, cover and refrigerate at least 1 hour.)

Heat oven to 350°. Divide dough into 8 equal parts. Shape each part into strip, 8x1½ inches, on ungreased cookie sheet. Make slight indentation down center of each with handle of wooden spoon; fill with about 1½ teaspoons jam. Bake until edges are light brown, 10 to 12 minutes. Cool slightly. Drizzle with Almond Glaze. Cut diagonally into 1-inch pieces. *About 5 dozen bars.*

ALMOND GLAZE

Beat 1 cup powdered sugar, ½ teaspoon almond extract and 2 to 3 teaspoons water until smooth and of desired consistency.

Apricot Jam Strips: Substitute ½ cup apricot jam for the raspberry jam.

Raspberry Jam Strips

Almond-Toffee Triangles

1 cup margarine or butter, softened	1 teaspoon vanilla
½ cup granulated sugar	2 cups all-purpose flour
½ cup packed brown sugar	¼ teaspoon salt
1 egg	¾ cup almond brickle chips

Heat oven to 350°. Mix margarine, sugars, egg and vanilla. Stir in flour and salt. Press dough in ungreased jelly roll pan, 15½x10½x1 inch, with floured hands. Sprinkle with brickle chips; press lightly. Bake until light brown, about 25 minutes. Cool 10 minutes. Cut into 2½-inch squares; cut each square diagonally into halves. Immediately remove from pan.   *About 4 dozen bars.*

Almond-Cardamom Triangles: Add 1 teaspoon ground cardamom with the flour and salt. Substitute ½ cup toasted diced almonds for the brickle chips.

Chocolate-Spice Triangles: Add 1 teaspoon ground cinnamon with the flour and salt. Substitute 1 package (12 ounces) semisweet chocolate chips for the brickle chips.

Macadamia Nut Triangles: Add 1 teaspoon ground ginger with the flour and salt. Substitute ½ cup chopped salted macadamia nuts for the brickle chips.

These bar cookies stack up well for holiday mailings. See page 171 for hints on packing cookies.

Chocolate-Almond Meringue Bars

½ cup granulated sugar	¼ teaspoon salt
½ cup packed brown sugar	1 package (6 ounces) semisweet chocolate chips
¾ cup margarine or butter, softened	1 cup flaked or shredded coconut
3 eggs, separated	½ cup chopped almonds
1 teaspoon vanilla	1 cup packed brown sugar
2 cups all-purpose flour	½ cup chopped almonds
1 teaspoon baking powder	
¼ teaspoon baking soda	

Beat granulated sugar, ½ cup brown sugar, the margarine, egg yolks and vanilla on low speed until blended. Beat on medium speed, scraping bowl constantly, until smooth, about 2 minutes. Stir in flour, baking powder, baking soda and salt. Press dough in greased baking pan, 13x9x2 inches, with floured hands; sprinkle with chocolate chips, coconut and ½ cup almonds.

Heat oven to 350°. Beat egg whites until foamy. Beat in 1 cup brown sugar, 1 tablespoon at a time; continue beating until stiff and glossy. Spread over mixture in pan; sprinkle with ½ cup almonds. Bake until meringue is set and light brown, 35 to 40 minutes. Cool; cut into bars, about 2 x 1 inch.   *About 4 dozen bars.*

Chocolate-Caramel Crunch Bars

1 package (14 ounces) caramels (about 48)	1 cup margarine or butter, melted
⅓ cup water	½ teaspoon baking soda
2 cups all-purpose flour	¼ teaspoon salt
2 cups quick-cooking oats	1 package (6 ounces) semisweet chocolate chips
1 cup packed brown sugar	

Heat caramels and water over low heat, stirring frequently, until caramels are melted and mixture is smooth.

Heat oven to 350°. Mix flour, oats, brown sugar, margarine, baking soda and salt. Reserve 1 cup mixture for topping. Press remaining mixture in ungreased baking pan, 13x9x2 inches. Bake 10 minutes.

Sprinkle baked layer with chocolate chips; drizzle with caramel mixture. Sprinkle with reserved crumbly mixture. Bake until light brown, about 15 minutes. Cool slightly. Cut into bars, 2x1 inch. *4 dozen bars.*

☐ **Microwave Tip:** Place caramels and water in 4-cup glass measure. Microwave uncovered on high (100%) 2 minutes; stir. Microwave until caramels can be stirred smooth, 1 to 2 minutes longer.

Glazed Fruit Bars

1 cup sugar	½ teaspoon salt
⅓ cup shortening	½ teaspoon ground cinnamon
⅓ cup margarine or butter, softened	½ teaspoon ground nutmeg
1 egg	1 cup raisins
1 tablespoon grated orange peel, if desired	1 cup cut-up mixed candied fruit
¼ cup orange or pineapple juice	½ cup chopped nuts, if desired
2½ cups all-purpose flour	Powdered Sugar Glaze (below)
1 teaspoon baking soda	

Heat oven to 400°. Mix sugar, shortening, margarine, egg, orange peel and orange juice. Stir in remaining ingredients except Powdered Sugar Glaze. Spread in greased jelly roll pan, 15½x10½x1 inch. Bake until top springs back when touched, about 15 minutes; cool slightly. Spread with glaze. Decorate with bits of candied fruit if desired. Cut into bars, 2x1 inch. *About 5 dozen bars.*

POWDERED SUGAR GLAZE

Beat 1½ cups powdered sugar, ¼ teaspoon vanilla and 2 to 3 tablespoons milk until smooth and of desired consistency.

Glazed Date-Raisin Bars: Substitute 1 cup cut-up dates for the candied fruit.

Glazed Orange-Raisin Bars: Substitute 1 cup snipped candied orange slices (about 13) for the candied fruit.

Opposite: Several sweet ways to say ''Merry Christmas.'' Clockwise from top: Chocolate-Peppermint Pretzels (page 15), Turtle Cookies (page 16), Coconut-Pecan Balls (page 18), Glazed Fruit Bars and Chocolate-Caramel Crunch Bars (both this page)

Pecan-Cheesecake Squares

1 cup all-purpose flour
⅓ cup margarine or butter, softened
¼ cup packed brown sugar
1 package (8 ounces) cream cheese, softened

⅓ cup packed brown sugar
1 egg
2 teaspoons milk
½ teaspoon vanilla
¼ cup finely chopped pecans

Heat oven to 350°. Mix flour, margarine and ¼ cup brown sugar; press in ungreased baking pan, 8x8x2 inches. Bake 10 minutes.

Beat remaining ingredients except pecans in small mixer bowl on low speed, scraping bowl constantly, 30 seconds. Beat on medium speed, scraping bowl occasionally, 1 minute. Spread over baked layer; sprinkle with pecans. Bake until edges are light brown, about 25 minutes. Cool; refrigerate at least 2 hours. Cut into 1¼-inch squares. Store in refrigerator. *About 3 dozen squares.*

Cherry-Cheesecake Squares: Substitute ¼ cup granulated sugar for the ⅓ cup brown sugar and stir ⅓ cup cut-up candied cherries into cheese mixture before pouring over baked layer.

Toffee-Coconut Bars

½ cup packed brown sugar
¼ cup margarine or butter, softened
¼ cup shortening

1 cup all-purpose flour
Coconut-Almond Topping or Coconut-Lemon Topping (below)

Heat oven to 350°. Mix brown sugar, margarine and shortening. Stir in flour. Press in ungreased baking pan, 13x9x2 inches. Bake 10 minutes. Spread Coconut-Almond Topping over baked layer. Bake until golden brown, about 25 minutes; cool slightly. Cut into bars, 2 x 1 inch. *About 4 dozen bars.*

COCONUT-ALMOND TOPPING

2 eggs
1 cup packed brown sugar
1 cup shredded coconut
1 cup chopped almonds

2 tablespoons flour
1 teaspoon baking powder
1 teaspoon vanilla
½ teaspoon salt

Beat eggs; stir in remaining ingredients.

COCONUT-LEMON TOPPING

2 eggs
1 cup packed brown sugar
1 teaspoon grated lemon peel
2 tablespoons lemon juice

½ teaspoon salt
1 cup shredded coconut
1 cup cut-up raisins
1 cup chopped walnuts

Beat eggs; stir in remaining ingredients.

Chocolate-Coconut Squares

1¾ cups graham cracker
    crumbs (20 squares)
½ cup margarine or butter,
    melted
2 tablespoons sugar
2 cups flaked coconut
1 can (14 ounces) sweetened
    condensed milk

¼ teaspoon almond extract or
    1 teaspoon vanilla
1 package (12 ounces)
    semisweet chocolate
    chips
¼ cup toasted diced almonds,
    if desired

Heat oven to 350°. Mix cracker crumbs, margarine and sugar. Press in ungreased baking pan, 13x9x2 inches. Bake 10 minutes. Mix coconut, milk and almond extract; spread over baked layer. Bake 15 minutes.

Sprinkle chocolate chips over baked layer. Bake just until chocolate is melted, 1 to 2 minutes. Spread chocolate over top; sprinkle with almonds. Cool completely. Cut into 1½-inch squares. Store in refrigerator. *About 4 dozen squares.*

Quick Praline Bars

24 graham cracker squares
½ cup packed brown sugar
½ cup margarine or butter

½ teaspoon vanilla
½ cup chopped pecans

Heat oven to 350°. Arrange graham crackers in single layer in ungreased jelly roll pan, 15½x10½x1 inch. Heat brown sugar and margarine to boiling; boil and stir 1 minute. Remove from heat. Stir in vanilla. Pour over crackers; spread evenly. Sprinkle with pecans. Bake until bubbly, 8 to 10 minutes. Cool slightly. Cut into bars, 2¼x1¼ inches. *About 4 dozen bars.*

Lime Squares

1 cup all-purpose flour
½ cup margarine or butter,
    softened
¼ cup powdered sugar
1 cup granulated sugar
2 eggs

2 tablespoons flour
2 teaspoons grated lime peel
2 tablespoons lime juice
½ teaspoon baking powder
¼ teaspoon salt
2 or 3 drops green food color

Heat oven to 350°. Mix flour, margarine and powdered sugar. Press in ungreased baking pan, 8x8x2 or 9x9x2 inches, building up ½-inch edges. Bake 20 minutes.

Beat remaining ingredients until light and fluffy, about 3 minutes; pour over baked layer. Bake until no indentation remains when touched in center, about 25 minutes. Cool; sprinkle with powdered sugar if desired. Cut into 1-inch squares. *About 4 dozen squares.*

Lime Squares

Holiday Cookie Mix

8 cups all-purpose flour
4 cups packed brown sugar
1 tablespoon salt

1½ teaspoons baking soda
1½ cups shortening

Mix flour, brown sugar, salt and baking soda. Cut in shortening until mixture resembles fine crumbs. Place desired amounts of mix in storage containers. Seal tightly, label and refrigerate no longer than 10 weeks. To measure, dip dry measuring cup into cookie mix; level with straight-edged spatula.   *15 to 16 cups cookie mix.*

Note: Large roasting pan, plastic dishpan, vegetable bin or 6-quart mixing bowl can be used for mixing ingredients. Plastic containers, jars or large plastic bags can be used to store cookie mix.

Toffee Bars

4 cups cookie mix (above)
½ cup margarine or butter, softened
1 egg
1 teaspoon vanilla

1 bar (4 ounces) milk chocolate candy, broken into sections
½ cup chopped nuts, if desired

Heat oven to 350°. Mix cookie mix, margarine, egg and vanilla. Press in greased baking pan, 13x9x2 inches.

Bake until very light brown, 25 to 30 minutes (crust will be soft). Remove from oven; immediately place pieces of chocolate candy on baked layer. Let stand until soft; spread evenly. Sprinkle with nuts. Cut into bars, about 2x1 inch, while warm.   *4 dozen bars.*

Spice-Raisin Cookies

4 cups cookie mix (above)
1 cup raisins
¼ cup molasses
1 egg
1 teaspoon ground ginger
½ teaspoon ground cinnamon

½ teaspoon ground cloves
½ teaspoon ground nutmeg
3 tablespoons water
Vanilla Butter Frosting (below)

Heat oven to 375°. Mix cookie mix, raisins, molasses, egg, ginger, cinnamon, cloves and nutmeg. Stir in water. Drop dough by teaspoonfuls onto ungreased cookie sheet. Bake until almost no indentation remains when touched, about 9 minutes. Immediately remove from cookie sheet; cool. Frost with Vanilla Butter Frosting. *4 dozen cookies.*

VANILLA BUTTER FROSTING
Mix 3 cups powdered sugar, ⅓ cup margarine or butter, softened, and 1½ teaspoons vanilla. Beat in about 2 tablespoons milk until smooth and of spreading consistency.

Opposite: Holiday temptations from a homemade cookie mix. Clockwise from jar of Holiday Cookie Mix (this page): Toffee Bars (this page), Cherry-Coconut Bars (page 32), Fruit Jumbles (page 33), Chocolate Bonbon Cookies and Sparkle Cookies (both page 32)

Cherry-Coconut Bars

4 cups cookie mix (page 31)
½ cup margarine or butter,
   softened
3 eggs, beaten
1½ cups sugar
⅓ cup all-purpose flour
¾ teaspoon baking powder
½ teaspoon salt
1 teaspoon vanilla
¾ cup flaked coconut
¾ cup chopped maraschino
   cherries, drained
1 cup chopped nuts

Heat oven to 350°. Mix cookie mix and margarine; press in ungreased baking pan, 13x9x2 inches. Bake 25 minutes. Mix remaining ingredients except nuts; spread over baked layer. Sprinkle with nuts. Bake 25 minutes. Cool completely. Cut into bars, about 2x1 inch.   *4 dozen bars.*

Chocolate Bonbon Cookies

4 cups cookie mix (page 31)
¼ cup margarine or butter,
   softened
2 eggs
2 ounces melted unsweetened
   chocolate (cool)
1 teaspoon vanilla
½ teaspoon almond extract
1 cup chopped nuts
Powdered sugar
Easy Frosting (below)
Coconut, nuts, colored
   sugar or candied or
   maraschino cherries, if
   desired

Heat oven to 375°. Mix cookie mix, margarine, eggs, chocolate, vanilla, almond extract and nuts. Shape dough into 1-inch balls. Place about 1 inch apart on ungreased cookie sheet. Bake until set, 10 to 12 minutes. Cool slightly before removing from cookie sheet.

Roll about 30 cookies in powdered sugar while warm; cool. Roll in powdered sugar again. Frost remaining cookies with Easy Frosting. Decorate frosted cookies with coconut, nuts, colored sugar or cherries.   *5 dozen cookies.*

EASY FROSTING
Beat 1 cup powdered sugar, ½ teaspoon almond extract and about 1 tablespoon milk until smooth and of spreading consistency.

Sparkle Cookies

4 cups cookie mix (page 31)
⅓ cup margarine or butter,
   softened
2 eggs
1½ teaspoons cream of tartar
½ teaspoon baking soda
½ teaspoon almond extract
Red and green sugar

Heat oven to 400°. Mix all ingredients except red and green sugar. Shape dough by teaspoonfuls into balls. Roll in sugar. Place balls about 2 inches apart on ungreased cookie sheet. Bake until light brown, 8 to 10 minutes. Immediately remove from cookie sheet; cool.   *4 dozen cookies.*

Fruit Jumbles

4 cups cookie mix (page 31)
¾ cup dairy sour cream
2 eggs
1 teaspoon vanilla
1½ cups candied cherries, cut
    into halves

1½ cups cut-up dates
1 cup chopped pecans
    Pecan halves, if desired

Heat oven to 375°. Mix cookie mix, sour cream, eggs and vanilla. Stir in cherries, dates and chopped pecans. Drop dough by rounded teaspoonfuls about 2 inches apart onto ungreased cookie sheet. Place pecan half on each cookie. Bake until almost no indentation remains when touched, about 8 minutes. Immediately remove from cookie sheet; cool.   *6 dozen cookies.*

Festive Cheese Tarts

12 vanilla wafers (1½-inch size)
1 package (8 ounces) cream
    cheese, softened
¼ cup sugar
1 egg

1 teaspoon milk
1 teaspoon vanilla
    Red and green maraschino or
        candied cherries, cut up

Heat oven to 350°. Place 12 miniature foil baking cups, 2x1 inch, on cookie sheet. Place a vanilla wafer in each. Beat cream cheese, sugar, egg, milk and vanilla on low speed 30 seconds. Beat on medium speed until smooth, about 1 minute. Place 2 tablespoons mixture in each cup. Bake until set, 13 to 15 minutes. Cool. Garnish each tart with cherry pieces. Store in refrigerator.   *1 dozen tarts.*

Caramel-Pecan Tarts

1 cup all-purpose flour
½ cup margarine or butter,
    softened
¼ cup powdered sugar
¾ cup packed brown sugar
1 tablespoon margarine or
    butter, softened

1 egg, slightly beaten
1 teaspoon vanilla
¼ teaspoon salt
½ cup chopped pecans

Heat oven to 350°. Mix flour, ½ cup margarine and the powdered sugar. Divide into 24 equal pieces. Press each piece against bottom and side of ungreased small muffin cup, 1¾x1 inch. Do not allow pastry to extend above tops of cups.

Mix remaining ingredients. Spoon scant tablespoon mixture into each muffin cup. Bake until filling is set and crust is light brown, about 20 minutes. Cool in muffin cups 20 minutes. Remove from muffin cups with tip of knife; cool on wire rack.   *2 dozen tarts.*

Spritz

1 cup margarine or butter, softened	1 teaspoon almond extract or vanilla
½ cup sugar	½ teaspoon salt
2¼ cups all-purpose flour	1 egg

Heat oven to 400°. Mix margarine and sugar. Stir in remaining ingredients. Fill cookie press with dough; form desired shapes on ungreased cookie sheet. Bake until set but not brown, 6 to 9 minutes. *About 5 dozen cookies.*

Butter-Rum Spritz: Substitute rum flavoring for the almond extract. Tint parts of dough with different food colors. After baking, glaze cooled cookies with Butter-Rum Glaze: Heat ¼ cup margarine or butter over low heat until melted; remove from heat. Stir in 1 cup powdered sugar and 1 teaspoon rum flavoring. Beat in 1 to 2 tablespoons hot water until of desired consistency.

Chocolate Spritz: Stir 2 ounces melted unsweetened chocolate (cool) into margarine mixture.

Christmas Decorated Spritz: Before baking, top cookies with currants, raisins, candies, nuts, slices of candied fruits or candied fruit peels arranged in colorful and attractive patterns. Or, after baking, decorate with colored sugar, nonpareils, red cinnamon candies or finely chopped nuts; use a drop of corn syrup to hold decorations on cookies.

Holly Wreaths: Using star plate, hold press in semi-horizontal position and form wreaths by moving press in a circular motion. Gently push ends of dough together to form wreaths. Use bits of red and green candied cherries to form holly berries and leaves.

Molasses Spritz

1 cup packed brown sugar	1½ teaspoons ground ginger
1 cup shortening	1 teaspoon ground cinnamon
1 cup molasses	½ teaspoon baking soda
1 egg	
3½ cups all-purpose flour	

Heat oven to 375°. Mix brown sugar, shortening, molasses and egg. Stir in flour, ginger, cinnamon and baking soda. Divide dough into 4 equal parts; fill cookie press with 1 part dough. Press into long strips about 2 inches apart on greased cookie sheet. Repeat with remaining dough. Bake until edges begin to brown, 8 to 10 minutes. Cut each strip into 3-inch pieces while warm. Remove from cookie sheet; cool. *About 11 dozen cookies.*

Spritz

Cream Cheese Cookie Wreaths

1 cup margarine or butter, softened	½ cup sugar
1 package (3 ounces) cream cheese, softened	1 teaspoon vanilla
	2 cups all-purpose flour
	Candied cherries

Heat oven to 375°. Mix margarine and cream cheese. Stir in remaining ingredients except candied cherries. Fill cookie press with dough. Using star plate, hold press in semi-horizontal position and form wreaths on ungreased cookie sheet by moving press in a circular motion. Gently push ends of dough together to form wreaths. Use bits of red and green candied cherries to form holly berries and leaves. *About 4 dozen cookies.*

Krumkake

4 eggs	⅓ cup whipping cream
1 cup sugar	1 teaspoon vanilla
½ cup margarine or butter, melted	¾ cup all-purpose flour
	2 teaspoons cornstarch

Heat ungreased krumkake iron over medium-high heat on smallest surface unit of electric or gas range. Beat all ingredients until smooth. Test iron with few drops of water; if they skitter around, iron is correct temperature.

Drop ½ tablespoon batter on iron; close gently. Bake until light golden brown, about 15 seconds on each side. Keep iron over heat at all times. Remove cookie with knife. Immediately roll around roller. (An old-fashioned wooden clothespin or handle of a large wooden spoon works well.) *About 6 dozen cookies.*

Rosettes

Vegetable oil	1 teaspoon salt
2 eggs, slightly beaten	2 tablespoons vegetable oil
2 tablespoons granulated sugar	1 cup water or milk
	1 cup all-purpose flour

Heat oil (2 to 3 inches) in small deep saucepan to 400°. Mix eggs, sugar and salt in small deep bowl. Beat in remaining ingredients just until smooth. Heat rosette iron by placing in hot oil 1 minute. Tap excess oil from iron on paper towels; dip hot iron into batter *just* to top edge (don't go over top). Fry until golden brown, about 30 seconds. Immediately remove rosette; invert on paper towels to cool. (If rosette is not crisp, batter is too thick. Stir in a small amount of water or milk.)

Heat iron in hot oil and tap on paper towels before making each rosette. (If iron is not hot enough, batter will not stick.) Just before serving, sprinkle with powdered sugar. *About 3 dozen rosettes.*

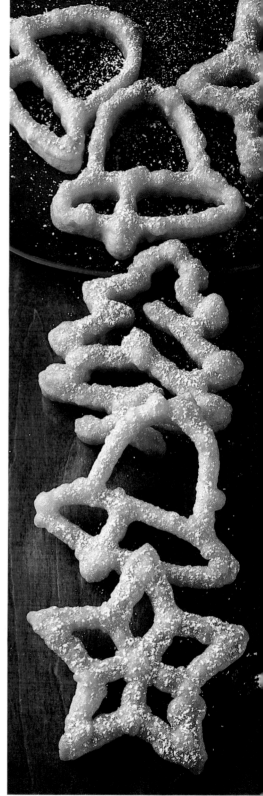

Rosettes

Easy Chocolate Fudge

Busy Santa's helpers can still find time to make this easy version of everyone's favorite candy.

1 cup granulated sugar	1 tablespoon light corn syrup
¼ cup cocoa	1 teaspoon vanilla
⅓ cup milk	⅓ cup chopped nuts
¼ cup margarine or butter	2 to 2¼ cups powdered sugar

Mix granulated sugar and cocoa in 2-quart saucepan. Stir in milk, margarine and corn syrup. Heat to boiling over medium heat, stirring frequently. Boil and stir 1 minute. Remove from heat; cool without stirring until bottom of pan is lukewarm, about 45 minutes. Stir in vanilla and nuts. Stir in powdered sugar until mixture is very stiff. Press in buttered loaf pan, 9x5x3 inches. Refrigerate until firm, about 30 minutes. Cut into 1-inch squares.   *32 candies.*

Walnut Caramels

1 can (14 ounces) sweetened condensed milk	1 teaspoon vanilla
1 cup light corn syrup	½ cup finely chopped walnuts
⅛ teaspoon salt	
2 tablespoons margarine or butter	

Line bottom and 2 sides of baking pan, 8x8x2 inches, with aluminum foil. Butter bottom foil. Heat milk, corn syrup and salt to boiling in heavy 1½-quart saucepan over medium heat, stirring constantly. Cook over medium heat, stirring frequently, until candy thermometer registers 245° or until small amount of mixture dropped into very cold water forms a firm ball. Stir in margarine, vanilla and walnuts. Immediately spread in pan; cool. Cut into 1x½-inch pieces.   *About 10 dozen candies.*

Toffee

1 cup chopped pecans	½ cup semisweet chocolate chips
¾ cup packed brown sugar	
½ cup margarine or butter	

Butter baking pan, 9x9x2 inches. Spread pecans in pan. Heat brown sugar and margarine to boiling, stirring constantly. Boil over medium heat, stirring constantly, 7 minutes. Immediately spread mixture over pecans in pan.

Sprinkle chocolate chips over hot mixture; place cookie sheet over pan until chocolate chips are melted. Spread melted chocolate over candy. Cut into about 1½-inch squares while hot. Refrigerate until firm.   *3 dozen candies.*

Peanut Brittle

1½ teaspoons baking soda
 1 teaspoon water
 1 teaspoon vanilla
1½ cups sugar
 1 cup water

 1 cup light corn syrup
 3 tablespoons margarine or
    butter
 1 pound shelled unroasted
    peanuts

Butter 2 cookie sheets, 15½x12 inches; keep warm. Mix baking soda, 1 teaspoon water and the vanilla; reserve. Mix sugar, 1 cup water and the corn syrup in 3-quart saucepan. Cook over medium heat, stirring occasionally, to 240° on candy thermometer or until small amount of syrup dropped into very cold water forms a soft ball that flattens when removed from water.

Stir in margarine and peanuts. Cook, stirring constantly, to 300° or until small amount of mixture dropped into very cold water separates into threads that are hard and brittle (watch carefully so mixture does not burn). Immediately remove from heat; stir in baking soda mixture.

Pour half of the candy mixture onto each cookie sheet and quickly spread about ¼ inch thick. Cool; break into pieces.   *2 pounds candy.*

Pecan Roll

 1 cup granulated sugar
 1 cup packed brown sugar
⅔ cup milk
 2 tablespoons corn syrup
¼ teaspoon salt

 2 tablespoons margarine or
    butter
 1 teaspoon vanilla
½ cup finely chopped pecans

Heat sugars, milk, corn syrup and salt in a 3-quart saucepan over medium heat, stirring constantly, until sugar is dissolved. Cook, stirring occasionally, to 234° on candy thermometer or until small amount of mixture dropped into very cold water forms a soft ball that flattens when removed from water. Remove from heat; add margarine.

Cool without stirring to 120° (bottom of pan will be lukewarm). Add vanilla; beat continuously with wooden spoon until candy is thick and no longer glossy, 5 to 10 minutes (mixture will hold its shape when dropped from spoon). Turn candy onto waxed paper and shape into 12-inch roll; roll in pecans. Wrap and refrigerate until firm. Cut into ¼-inch slices.   *About 4 dozen candies.*

No-Cook Divinity

1 package (7.2 ounces) fluffy white frosting mix	½ cup boiling water
⅓ cup light corn syrup	4 to 4½ cups powdered sugar
1 teaspoon vanilla	1 cup chopped nuts

Beat frosting mix (dry), corn syrup, vanilla and boiling water in small mixer bowl on high speed until stiff peaks form, about 5 minutes. Transfer to large mixer bowl; gradually beat in sugar on low speed. (It may be necessary to stir in the last cup of sugar by hand.) Stir in nuts.

Drop mixture by teaspoonfuls onto waxed paper. When outside of candy feels firm, turn over if necessary to dry bottoms of candies; let dry at least 12 hours. Store candy in airtight container. *About 5½ dozen candies.*

Candied Cherry Delights: Substitute 1 teaspoon almond extract for the vanilla and 1 cup chopped candied cherries for the nuts.

Peppy Mints: Substitute ½ teaspoon peppermint extract for the vanilla and, if desired, 1 cup crushed peppermint candy for the nuts. Tint with few drops food color if desired.

Spanish Crunch: Substitute dark corn syrup for the light and salted shelled Spanish peanuts for the nuts.

Chocolate-Coconut Candies

1 cup mashed potatoes	1 package (12 ounces) semisweet chocolate chips
1 pound powdered sugar (4 cups)	2 tablespoons shortening
1 teaspoon almond extract	
1 pound flaked coconut (about 4 cups)	

Mix mashed potatoes, powdered sugar and almond extract; stir in coconut. Drop mixture by rounded teaspoonfuls onto waxed paper; shape into balls. (If mixture is too soft to shape, refrigerate until firm, 30 to 60 minutes.) Heat chocolate chips and shortening over low heat, stirring frequently, until melted. Dip balls into chocolate with tongs until coated; place on waxed paper. Refrigerate until firm. *About 4 dozen candies.*

Cocoa Balls: Omit chocolate chips and shortening. Mix ¼ cup cocoa and ¼ cup sugar; coat coconut balls with cocoa mixture.

Coconut-Almond Candies: Shape coconut mixture around blanched almond for each candy.

Coconut Bars: Press coconut mixture in ungreased baking pan, 13x9x2 inches; spread with melted chocolate. Refrigerate until firm, 30 to 60 minutes. Cut into bars, 2x1 inch. *4 dozen bars.*

Opposite: Irresistible offerings from your candy kitchen. Top to bottom: No-Cook Divinity and Peppy Mints (both this page), Bourbon Balls (page 41), Pecan Roll slices (page 37) and Peanut Butter Bonbons (page 40)

Brandied Stuffed Dates

1 pound pitted dates
1 cup brandy

1 cup pecan halves
Sugar, if desired

Soak dates in brandy, turning occasionally, until most of the brandy is absorbed, about 24 hours. Place a pecan half in each date; press to close. Roll in sugar. Store in airtight container in refrigerator.

Peanut Butter Squares

1½ cups powdered sugar
1 cup graham cracker
    crumbs (about
    12 squares)
½ cup margarine or butter

½ cup peanut butter
1 package (6 ounces)
    semisweet chocolate
    chips

Mix powdered sugar and cracker crumbs. Heat margarine and peanut butter over low heat until melted; stir into crumb mixture. Press in ungreased baking pan, 8x8x2 inches. Heat chocolate chips in small saucepan over low heat, stirring frequently, until melted. Spread over crumb mixture. Refrigerate until firm, about 30 minutes. Cut into 1-inch squares. *3 dozen candies.*

Peanut Butter Bonbons: Shape mixture into 1-inch balls. Heat chocolate chips with 1 tablespoon shortening. Dip balls into chocolate with tongs until coated; place on waxed paper. Refrigerate until firm.

Fudge Meltaways

Fudge Meltaways

1¾ cups graham cracker
    crumbs (about
    20 squares)
1 cup flaked coconut
¼ cup cocoa
2 tablespoons granulated
    sugar
½ cup margarine or butter,
    melted

2 tablespoons water
2 cups powdered sugar
¼ cup margarine or butter,
    softened
2 tablespoons milk
1 teaspoon vanilla

Mix cracker crumbs, coconut, cocoa and granulated sugar. Stir in ½ cup margarine and the water. Press in ungreased baking pan, 9x9x2 inches. Refrigerate while making frosting.

Mix remaining ingredients. (If necessary, stir in 1 to 2 teaspoons additional milk for spreading consistency.) Spread over crumb mixture. Refrigerate 1 hour. Cut into 1-inch squares. Decorate with cut-up red and green candied cherries if desired. *About 5 dozen squares.*

Bourbon Balls

3 cups finely crushed vanilla
   wafers (about 75)
2 cups powdered sugar
1 cup finely chopped pecans
   or walnuts (about
   4 ounces)

¼ cup cocoa
½ cup bourbon
¼ cup light corn syrup
   Granulated or powdered
   sugar

Mix crushed wafers, powdered sugar, pecans and cocoa. Stir in bourbon and corn syrup. Shape mixture into 1-inch balls. Roll in granulated sugar. Refrigerate in tightly covered container several days before serving. *About 5 dozen candies.*

Brandy Balls: Substitute ½ cup brandy for the bourbon.

Rum Balls: Substitute ½ cup light rum for the bourbon.

A perfect present: Pack in a pretty glass or jar and seal tightly.

Nutty O's

½ cup packed brown sugar
½ cup dark corn syrup
¼ cup margarine or butter
½ teaspoon salt

6 cups toasted oat cereal
1 cup pecan halves, walnut
   halves or peanuts
½ cup slivered almonds

Heat oven to 325°. Butter jelly roll pan, 15½x10½x1 inch. Heat brown sugar, corn syrup, margarine and salt in 3-quart saucepan over medium heat, stirring constantly, until sugar is dissolved, about 5 minutes. Remove from heat; stir in cereal and nuts until well coated. Spread in pan. Bake 15 minutes. Cool 10 minutes; loosen with metal spatula. Let stand until firm, about 1 hour. Store in covered container. *About 8 cups snack.*

Nutty Cereal Squares

4 cups toasted oat, crispy corn
   puff, corn flake or whole
   wheat flake cereal
1 cup salted peanuts
1 cup flaked coconut, if
   desired

1 cup sugar
1 cup half-and-half
½ cup light corn syrup

Mix cereal, peanuts and coconut in buttered 4-quart bowl. Cook sugar, half-and-half and corn syrup over medium heat, stirring occasionally, to 236° on candy thermometer or until small amount of mixture dropped into very cold water forms a soft ball that flattens when removed from water.

Pour over cereal mixture; stir until well coated. Pat evenly in buttered baking pan, 9x9x2 inches, with buttered back of spoon. Cool; cut into 2-inch squares. *About 16 squares.*

Marshmallow Bars

32 large marshmallows or
   3 cups miniature
   marshmallows
¼ cup margarine or butter

½ teaspoon vanilla
5 cups crispy corn puff,
   toasted oat, corn flake or
   whole wheat flake cereal

Heat marshmallows and margarine in 3-quart saucepan over low heat, stirring constantly, until marshmallows are melted and mixture is smooth. Remove from heat; stir in vanilla. Stir in half of the cereal at a time until evenly coated. Press in buttered baking pan, 9x9x2 inches. Cool. Cut into bars, 2x1 inch. *About 3 dozen bars.*

Chocolate-Marshmallow Bars: Heat 1 package (6 ounces) semi-sweet chocolate chips in heavy saucepan over low heat, stirring frequently, until melted; spread over cereal mixture in pan.

Coconutty-Marshmallow Bars: Substitute ½ cup flaked coconut and ½ cup coarsely chopped nuts for 1 cup of the cereal.

Gumdrop-Marshmallow Bars: Stir in ¼ teaspoon ground cinnamon with the vanilla. Add 1 cup small gumdrops, cut into halves, with the cereal.

Peanut Butter-Marshmallow Bars: Stir ½ cup peanut butter into marshmallow-margarine mixture until melted.

Gumdrop-Marshmallow Bars

Caramel-Coconut Snack

8 cups crispy corn puff cereal
2 cups shredded coconut
1 cup packed brown sugar
½ cup light corn syrup

½ teaspoon salt
¼ cup margarine or butter
2 teaspoons vanilla
¼ teaspoon baking soda

Heat oven to 200°. Mix cereal and coconut in broiler pan. Heat brown sugar, corn syrup and salt to boiling, stirring occasionally. Boil 2 minutes, stirring frequently. Remove from heat; stir in margarine, vanilla and baking soda. Pour over cereal mixture; stir until well coated. Bake 1 hour. Cool on waxed paper.   *10 cups snack.*

Oven Caramel Corn

15 cups popped corn
1 cup packed brown sugar
½ cup margarine or butter

¼ cup light corn syrup
½ teaspoon salt
½ teaspoon baking soda

Heat oven to 200°. Divide popped corn between 2 ungreased baking pans, 13x9x2 inches. Heat brown sugar, margarine, corn syrup and salt to simmering over medium-high heat, stirring constantly. Cook, stirring occasionally, 5 minutes. Remove from heat; stir in baking soda. Pour over popped corn; stir until well coated. Bake 1 hour, stirring every 15 minutes.   *About 15 cups snack.*

Nutty Caramel Corn: Decrease popped corn to 12 cups. Add 1½ cups walnut or pecan halves and/or unblanched whole almonds to each pan of popped corn before stirring.

Popcorn Balls

½ cup sugar
½ cup light corn syrup
¼ cup margarine or butter

½ teaspoon salt
Few drops food color
8 cups popped corn

Heat sugar, corn syrup, margarine, salt and food color to simmering in 4-quart Dutch oven over medium-high heat, stirring constantly. Add popped corn. Cook, stirring constantly, until popcorn is well coated, about 3 minutes. Cool slightly.

Dip hands into cold water; shape mixture into 2½-inch balls. Place on waxed paper; cool completely. Wrap individually in plastic wrap or place in plastic bags and tie.   *8 or 9 popcorn balls.*

Caramel Popcorn Balls: Substitute packed brown sugar for the sugar and dark corn syrup for the light; omit food color.

Chocolate Popcorn Balls: Add 2 tablespoons cocoa with the sugar and omit food color.

Desserts

Whether it's the grand finale to the Christmas feast or a hearty refreshment for a crowd of carolers, you'll find happy endings here for every holiday occasion. Because we know how busy you are this time of year, there are plenty of do-ahead recipes, and for gatherings of clan or kindred spirits, desserts of generous portions. Children will love the cheery decorated cakes (perfect for holiday birthdays too). And to evoke Christmas past for everyone, recall these delicious traditions: fruitcakes and mincemeat pies; an elegant Bûche de Noël; cloudlike trifles; and a rich steamed pudding, to set gloriously ablaze.

Christmas Coconut Cake

2 cups all-purpose flour	4 egg whites
1½ cups granulated sugar	⅔ cup flaked coconut
3½ teaspoons baking powder	Tutti-Frutti Filling (below)
1 teaspoon salt	1 cup whipping cream
½ cup shortening	¼ cup powdered sugar
1 cup milk	¾ teaspoon almond extract
1 teaspoon vanilla	

Heat oven to 350°. Grease and flour 2 round layer pans, 9x1½ inches. Beat flour, granulated sugar, baking powder, salt, shortening, milk and vanilla in large mixer bowl on low speed, scraping bowl constantly, 30 seconds. Beat on high speed, scraping bowl occasionally, 2 minutes. Add egg whites; beat on high speed, scraping bowl occasionally, 2 minutes. Stir in coconut. Pour into pans.

Bake until wooden pick inserted in center comes out clean, 30 to 35 minutes; cool. Fill layers and frost top of cake to within 1 inch of edge with filling. Beat whipping cream, powdered sugar and almond extract in chilled bowl until stiff. Spread side and top edge of cake with whipped cream. Refrigerate.

TUTTI-FRUTTI FILLING

2 egg yolks	½ to 1 cup finely chopped
⅔ cup dairy sour cream	raisins
⅔ cup sugar	½ to 1 cup finely chopped
1 cup finely chopped pecans	candied cherries
⅔ cup flaked coconut	

Mix egg yolks and sour cream in saucepan; stir in sugar. Cook over low heat, stirring constantly, until mixture begins to simmer. Simmer, stirring constantly, until mixture begins to thicken. Remove from heat; stir in remaining ingredients. Cool.

Cherry Angel Food Cake

1 package (15 or 16 ounces)
    white angel food cake
    mix
1½ cups whipping cream
⅓ cup powdered sugar

12 well-drained maraschino
    cherries, cut up
2 tablespoons maraschino
    cherry syrup
⅓ cup chopped walnuts

Bake cake mix as directed on package. Cool. Beat whipping cream and powdered sugar in chilled bowl until stiff. Fold in cherries, cherry syrup and walnuts. Frost cake. Refrigerate.

Spicy Angel Food Cake

1 package (15 ounces)
    traditional white angel
    food cake mix
1 teaspoon pumpkin pie
    spice

1½ cups whipping cream
⅓ cup packed brown sugar
1 teaspoon vanilla

Prepare cake mix as directed on package except—add pie spice with Packet 2 (Cake Flour Mix). Bake as directed. Cool; remove from pan. Beat whipping cream, brown sugar and vanilla in chilled bowl until stiff; frost cake. Refrigerate.

Minted Angel Allegretti

1 package (15 or 16 ounces)
    white angel food cake
    mix
2¼ cups miniature
    marshmallows
½ cup milk
¼ cup white or green crème
    de menthe

¼ teaspoon salt
6 to 10 drops green food color
2 cups whipping cream
1 square (1 ounce)
    unsweetened chocolate
¼ teaspoon shortening

Bake cake mix as directed on package. Cool. Split cake to make 3 layers.

Heat marshmallows and milk over medium heat, stirring occasionally, until marshmallows are melted, about 5 minutes; remove from heat. Cool at room temperature until thickened, 20 to 25 minutes. Stir in crème de menthe, salt and food color.

Beat whipping cream in chilled bowl until stiff. Fold into marshmallow mixture. Stack cake layers, spreading top of each with 1 cup of the filling. Frost side of cake with remaining filling. Heat chocolate and shortening until melted; drizzle chocolate mixture by teaspoonfuls around top edge of cake, allowing it to run down side. Refrigerate until serving time.

Minted Angel Allegretti

Chocolate Nesselrode Cake

2 cups all-purpose flour
2 cups sugar
1 teaspoon baking soda
1 teaspoon salt
½ teaspoon baking powder
¾ cup water
¾ cup buttermilk

½ cup shortening
2 eggs
1 teaspoon vanilla
4 ounces melted unsweetened chocolate (cool)
Nesselrode Filling (below)
Cocoa Fluff (below)

Heat oven to 350°. Grease and flour three 8-inch round layer pans. Beat all ingredients except Nesselrode Filling and Cocoa Fluff in large mixer bowl on low speed, scraping bowl constantly, 30 seconds. Beat on high speed, scraping bowl occasionally, 3 minutes. Pour into pans. Bake until wooden pick inserted in center comes out clean, 30 to 35 minutes. Cool. Fill layers and frost top of cake with Nesselrode Filling. Frost side of cake with Cocoa Fluff. Refrigerate.

NESSELRODE FILLING
Beat 1 cup whipping cream and ¼ cup powdered sugar in chilled bowl until stiff. Fold in ¼ cup Nesselrode.*

COCOA FLUFF
Beat 1 cup whipping cream, ¼ cup powdered sugar and 2 tablespoons cocoa in chilled bowl until stiff.

*¼ cup finely cut-up candied fruit and 1 teaspoon rum flavoring can be substituted for the Nesselrode.

Note: Cake can be baked in two 9-inch round layer pans. When cool, split to make 4 layers. Fill layers and frost top of cake with ¼ each of the Nesselrode Filling.

One of the traditional flavors of Christmastime, nesselrode was originally a pudding created by the chef to a 19th-century Russian count of the same name. Today a brandy- or rum-flavored mixture of candied fruits, chestnuts and raisins is often served as a dessert sauce.

Eggnog Cake

1 package (18.5 ounces) yellow cake mix with pudding
1 teaspoon rum flavoring
1 teaspoon ground nutmeg
¼ teaspoon ground ginger

1 package (15.4 ounces) creamy white frosting mix
3 tablespoons orange marmalade
Red and green food color

Grease and flour baking pan, 13x9x2 inches. Prepare cake mix as directed on package except—add rum flavoring, nutmeg and ginger before mixing. Pour into pan. Bake as directed. Invert on large tray or aluminum foil-covered cardboard; cool. Prepare frosting mix as directed on package except—heat the margarine over medium heat until delicate brown. Frost cake.

Mark 3 bells on top of cake with bell-shaped cookie cutter. Mix 2 tablespoons of the marmalade and 3 drops green food color. Mix remaining marmalade and 2 drops red food color. Fill 2 bells with green marmalade and 1 bell with red marmalade. Dip wooden pick into additional green food color and draw lines to connect bells.

Opposite: Chocolate Nesselrode Cake

Festive Cranberry Cake

1 package (18.5 ounces) white
 cake mix with pudding
2 cups whipping cream

¼ cup powdered sugar
1 jar (14 ounces) cranberry-
 orange relish

Bake cake in 2 layer pans, 8 or 9x1½ inches, as directed on package. Cool. Split cake to make 4 layers. Beat whipping cream and powdered sugar in chilled bowl until stiff. Reserve ½ cup cranberry-orange relish. Fold remaining relish into 1½ cups of the whipped cream; spread between cake layers. Spread reserved relish on top to within 1 inch of edge. Frost sides of cake and edge of top with remaining whipped cream. Refrigerate 1 to 2 hours before serving.

Bûche de Noël

In France, this beautiful cake log is traditionally featured at the réveillon, an elegant supper served after midnight Mass on Christmas Eve.

3 eggs
1 cup sugar
⅓ cup water
1 teaspoon vanilla
¾ cup all-purpose flour
1 teaspoon baking powder
¼ teaspoon salt
1 cup whipping cream

2 tablespoons sugar
1½ teaspoons powdered
 instant coffee
Cocoa Frosting (below)
Gumdrop Holly (page 51)
 or Meringue Mushrooms
 (page 167)

Heat oven to 375°. Line jelly roll pan, 15½x10½x1 inch, with aluminum foil or waxed paper; grease. Beat eggs in small mixer bowl on high speed until very thick and lemon colored, about 5 minutes. Pour eggs into large mixer bowl; gradually beat in 1 cup sugar. Beat in water and vanilla on low speed. Gradually add flour, baking powder and salt, beating just until batter is smooth. Pour into pan, spreading batter to corners. Bake until wooden pick inserted in center comes out clean, 12 to 15 minutes.

Loosen cake from edges of pan; immediately invert on towel generously sprinkled with powdered sugar. Remove foil; trim stiff edges of cake if necessary. While hot, roll cake and towel from narrow end. Cool on wire rack at least 30 minutes.

Beat whipping cream, 2 tablespoons sugar and the coffee in chilled bowl until stiff. Unroll cake; remove towel. Spread whipped cream mixture over cake. Roll up; frost with Cocoa Frosting. Make strokes with tines of fork to resemble bark. Decorate with Gumdrop Holly or Meringue Mushrooms. Store in refrigerator.   *10 servings.*

COCOA FROSTING

⅓ cup cocoa
⅓ cup margarine or butter,
 softened

2 cups powdered sugar
1½ teaspoons vanilla
1 to 2 tablespoons hot water

Mix cocoa and margarine. Stir in powdered sugar. Beat in vanilla and water until smooth and of spreading consistency.

Chocolate Ice-Cream Roll

¾ cup all-purpose flour
¼ cup cocoa
1 teaspoon baking powder
¼ teaspoon salt
3 eggs
1 cup granulated sugar

⅓ cup water
1 teaspoon vanilla
 Powdered sugar
1 pint peppermint, pistachio
  or cherry ice cream,
  slightly softened

Heat oven to 375°. Line jelly roll pan, 15½x10½x1 inch, with aluminum foil or waxed paper; grease. Mix flour, cocoa, baking powder and salt; reserve.

Beat eggs in small mixer bowl on high speed until very thick and lemon colored, 3 to 5 minutes. Pour eggs into large mixer bowl; gradually beat in granulated sugar. Beat in water and vanilla on low speed. Gradually add flour mixture, beating just until batter is smooth. Pour into pan, spreading batter to corners. Bake until wooden pick inserted in center comes out clean, 12 to 15 minutes.

Loosen cake from edges of pan; invert on towel generously sprinkled with powdered sugar. Carefully remove foil; trim stiff edges from cake if necessary. While hot, roll cake and towel from narrow end. Cool. Unroll cake and remove towel. Quickly spread ice cream over cake. Roll up and place seam side down on piece of aluminum foil. Wrap and freeze at least 4 hours. For longer storage, wrap and label; freeze no longer than 1 month. About 15 minutes before serving, remove roll from freezer; unwrap and sprinkle with powdered sugar.   *10 to 12 servings.*

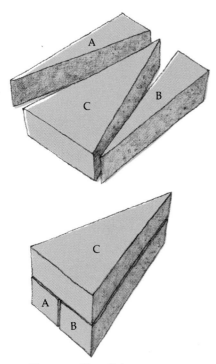

Christmas Tree Cake

Christmas Tree Cake

Heat oven to 350°. Grease and flour baking pan, 13x9x2 inches. Prepare 1 package (18.5 ounces) white or yellow cake mix with pudding as directed on package; pour into pan. Sprinkle batter with 2 tablespoons green sugar and 2 tablespoons multicolored nonpareils. Cut through batter with spatula to swirl. Bake as directed. Remove from pan; cool.

Cover large tray or piece of cardboard with aluminum foil or foil wrapping paper. Cut cake as shown in diagram. Prepare 1 package (7.2 ounces) fluffy white frosting mix as directed on package. Tint with 1 or 2 drops green food color. Arrange cake pieces A and B on tray to make tree shape (see diagram); frost. Place piece C on top; frost sides and top, making strokes through frosting to resemble tree branches.

Sprinkle cake with green sugar. Decorate with cut-up gumdrops. Insert 3 peppermint candy sticks in end of cake to make trunk.

Drum Cake

Bake your favorite 8- or 9-inch layer cake. Cool. Prepare 1 package (7.2 ounces) fluffy white frosting mix as directed on package. Tint with red food color if desired. Fill and frost cake.

Press striped peppermint candy sticks at angles into frosting around side of cake. Place a maraschino cherry at ends of sticks. Cross 2 candy sticks on top of cake for drumsticks if desired.

Christmas Snow Cake

Bake your favorite 8- or 9-inch layer cake. Cool. Prepare 1 package (7.2 ounces) fluffy white frosting mix as directed on package except—stir in ½ teaspoon almond extract. Fill and frost cake; sprinkle with flaked coconut.

Cut a paper circle the size of layer pan bottom. Draw a Christmas tree in center of paper; cut out tree. Place paper circle on cake. Sprinkle Tinted Coconut (below) in cutout area of circle. Fill base of tree with shaved chocolate. Remove circle. Decorate tree with red cinnamon candies. Roll red gumdrop on granulated sugar until flat; cut star for top of tree.

TINTED COCONUT
Mix 1 to 2 drops green food color and ½ teaspoon water. Place ½ cup flaked coconut and the food color mixture in tightly covered jar; shake until coconut is evenly tinted.

Note: For a Christmas birthday cake, insert small red candles in ring-shaped hard candies; press on tree branches.

Reindeer Cake

Bake any flavor layer cake mix in baking pan, 13x9x2 inches, as directed on package. Remove from pan and cool. Toast 1 cup flaked coconut in shallow baking pan in 350° oven, stirring frequently, until golden brown, about 5 minutes. Cut cake as shown in diagram. Arrange cake and pieces (ears) to form reindeer on aluminum foil-covered cardboard, 24x22 inches.

Prepare 1 package (7.2 ounces) fluffy white frosting mix as directed on package. Frost sides and top of cake, joining pieces together. Sprinkle toasted coconut over reindeer. Use large chocolate wafers for eyes, red gumdrop for nose, red shoestring licorice for mouth and antlers.

Snowman Cake

Grease and flour one 8- and one 9-inch round layer pan. Prepare any flavor layer cake mix as directed on package except—divide batter between pans (batter in pans should be same level). Bake as directed. Cool.

Prepare 1 package (7.2 ounces) fluffy white frosting mix as directed on package. Cover large tray or piece of cardboard with aluminum foil or foil wrapping paper. Arrange 8-inch layer for head of snowman and 9-inch layer for body on foil-covered tray. Frost layers, joining them together.

Sprinkle with flaked coconut. Use semisweet chocolate chips for buttons, large gumdrops for eyes and nose and red shoestring licorice for mouth and muffler. Place large chocolate wafer cookie on each side of head for earmuffs.

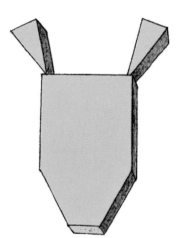

Reindeer Cake

Peppermint Bell Cake

Prepare your favorite white or yellow layer cake except—fold 1/3 cup crushed peppermint candy into batter. Bake in 2 round layer pans, 8 or 9x1½ inches, as directed. Fill and frost cake with 1 package (7.2 ounces) fluffy white frosting mix prepared as directed on package.

Coat side of cake with ½ to ¾ cup crushed peppermint candy, reserving 3 tablespoons for decoration. Draw outline of bells on top of cake or use cookie cutter. Outline bells using wooden pick dipped into red food color. Fill bells with reserved candy. Add Gumdrop Holly (below) and red cinnamon candies.

GUMDROP HOLLY
Roll green gumdrops about ⅛ inch thick on heavily sugared board; cut to resemble holly leaves.

Overleaf: Party-perfect decorated holiday cakes. Drum Cake, Peppermint Bell Cake, Snowman Cake, Christmas Tree Cake, Reindeer Cake and Christmas Snow Cake

Old-Fashioned Fruitcake

For best flavor, make fruitcakes 3 to 4 weeks in advance. Wine or brandy can be poured over the cakes before wrapping, or wrap them in wine- or brandy-soaked cloths.

3 cups all-purpose flour
1⅓ cups sugar
2 teaspoons salt
2 teaspoons ground cinnamon
1 teaspoon baking powder
1 teaspoon ground nutmeg
1 cup orange juice
1 cup vegetable oil
4 eggs
¼ cup dark molasses or dark corn syrup
15 ounces golden raisins (about 3 cups)

8 ounces pitted dates, cut into halves (1½ cups)
5 ounces whole red and green candied cherries (¾ cup)
5 ounces red and green candied pineapple, cut up (about 1 cup)
8 ounces whole Brazil nuts or pecan halves (1⅔ cups)
Sweet Glaze (below), if desired

Heat oven to 275°. Line 2 loaf pans, 9x5x3 or 8½x4½x2½ inches, with aluminum foil; grease. Beat all ingredients except fruits, nuts and Sweet Glaze in large mixer bowl on low speed, scraping bowl constantly, 30 seconds. Beat on medium speed, scraping bowl occasionally, 3 minutes. Stir in fruits and nuts. Spread in pans.

Bake until wooden pick inserted in center comes out clean, 2½ to 3 hours. If necessary, cover with aluminum foil during last hour of baking to prevent excessive browning. Remove from pans; cool. Wrap in plastic wrap or aluminum foil; store in refrigerator 3 to 4 weeks or freeze. Just before serving, drizzle with Sweet Glaze. *2 fruitcakes.*

SWEET GLAZE
Heat 2 tablespoons light corn syrup and 1 tablespoon water just to boiling; cool to lukewarm.

Jeweled Fruitcake

8 ounces dried apricots (about 2 cups)
8 ounces pitted dates (about 2 cups)
9 ounces Brazil nuts (about 1½ cups)
5 ounces red and green candied pineapple, cut up (about 1 cup)

1 cup red and green maraschino cherries
¾ cup all-purpose flour
¾ cup sugar
½ teaspoon baking powder
½ teaspoon salt
3 eggs
1½ teaspoons vanilla

Heat oven to 300°. Line loaf pan, 9x5x3 or 8½x4½x2½ inches, with aluminum foil; grease. Mix all ingredients; spread in pan. Bake until wooden pick inserted in center comes out clean, about 1¾ hours. If necessary, cover with aluminum foil during last 30 minutes of baking to prevent excessive browning. Remove from pan; cool. Wrap in plastic wrap; store in refrigerator.

Opposite: Jeweled Fruitcake

Cranberry Cake with Golden Sauce

2 cups all-purpose flour	1 teaspoon vanilla
1¼ cups sugar	½ teaspoon salt
1 cup milk	1 egg
2 tablespoons shortening	2 cups cranberries
2 teaspoons baking powder	Golden Sauce (below)

Heat oven to 350°. Grease and flour baking pan, 9x9x2 inches. Mix flour, sugar, milk, shortening, baking powder, vanilla, salt and egg; beat 30 seconds. Stir in cranberries. Pour into pan. Bake until wooden pick inserted in center comes out clean, 40 to 45 minutes. Serve warm with Golden Sauce.   *9 servings.*

GOLDEN SAUCE

Heat ½ cup sugar, ½ cup half-and-half, ½ cup margarine or butter and ½ teaspoon vanilla in 1-quart saucepan, stirring constantly, until margarine is melted.

Cinnamon-Apple Upside-Down Cake

Cinnamon-Apple Topping (below)	¾ cup milk
1¼ cups all-purpose flour	⅓ cup shortening
1 cup sugar	1 egg
1½ teaspoons baking powder	1 teaspoon vanilla
½ teaspoon salt	Sweetened Whipped Cream (below)

Prepare Cinnamon-Apple Topping. Heat oven to 350°. Beat remaining ingredients except Sweetened Whipped Cream in large mixer bowl on low speed, scraping bowl constantly, 30 seconds. Beat on high speed, scraping bowl occasionally, 3 minutes. Pour batter over Cinnamon-Apple Topping. Bake until wooden pick inserted in center comes out clean, 40 to 45 minutes. Immediately invert on heatproof serving plate; let pan remain a few minutes. Serve warm with Sweetened Whipped Cream.   *8 or 9 servings.*

CINNAMON-APPLE TOPPING

⅓ cup red cinnamon candies	1 tablespoon light corn syrup
2 tablespoons water	¼ cup packed brown sugar
2 tablespoons margarine or butter	2 medium apples, thinly sliced (about 2 cups)

Heat cinnamon candies, water, margarine and corn syrup over low heat, stirring occasionally, until candies are dissolved, 5 to 10 minutes. Pour cinnamon mixture into ungreased round layer pan, 9x1½ inches, or baking pan, 8x8x2 inches. Sprinkle brown sugar evenly over cinnamon mixture. Arrange apple slices in pan with edges overlapping.

SWEETENED WHIPPED CREAM

For 1 cup whipped cream: Beat ½ cup chilled whipping cream and 1 tablespoon granulated or powdered sugar in chilled bowl until stiff.

Butterscotch Meringue Cake

Velvet Crumb Cake
1 egg white
1 teaspoon lemon juice

½ cup packed brown sugar
½ cup chopped nuts
Ruby Glow Sauce (below)

Prepare Velvet Crumb Cake as directed on buttermilk baking mix package. During last few minutes of baking, beat egg white and lemon juice until foamy. Beat in brown sugar, 1 tablespoon at a time; continue beating until stiff and glossy.

Remove cake from oven. Spread with meringue; sprinkle with nuts. Increase oven temperature to 400°. Bake until meringue is brown, 8 to 10 minutes. Serve with Ruby Glow Sauce or, if desired, sweetened sliced strawberries. *8 or 9 servings*.

RUBY GLOW SAUCE

Mix ¼ cup sugar and 1 tablespoon cornstarch in 1-quart saucepan. Stir in ½ cup water and ½ cup whole cranberry sauce. Cook over medium heat, stirring constantly, until mixture thickens and boils. Boil and stir 1 minute. Stir in few drops red food color if desired.

Christmas Steamed Pudding

1 cup boiling water
1 cup chopped cranberries or
    cut-up raisins
2 tablespoons shortening
1½ cups all-purpose flour
½ cup sugar

1 teaspoon baking soda
1 teaspoon salt
½ cup molasses
1 egg
Creamy Sauce or Hard
    Sauce (below)

For a dramatic finale, dim the lights and flame the steamed pudding. Heat ¼ cup brandy in a tiny long-handled pan; ignite with a long fireplace match and pour over the warm unmolded pudding. The alcohol burns off, but the flavor remains. Or soak sugar cubes (enough to surround the unmolded pudding) in lemon extract. The cubes needn't touch; light just one.

Pour boiling water on cranberries; stir in shortening. Mix flour, sugar, baking soda and salt in 2-quart bowl. Stir in cranberry mixture, molasses and egg. Pour into well-greased 6-cup mold. Cover tightly with aluminum foil. Place mold on rack in Dutch oven or steamer; pour boiling water into Dutch oven halfway up mold. Cover Dutch oven. Keep water boiling over low heat until wooden pick inserted in center of pudding comes out clean, about 2 hours.

Remove mold from Dutch oven and let stand 5 minutes; unmold. Serve warm with Creamy Sauce or Hard Sauce. *8 servings*.

CREAMY SAUCE

Beat ½ cup powdered sugar and ½ cup margarine or butter, softened, in 1-quart saucepan until smooth and creamy. Stir in ½ cup whipping cream. Heat to boiling, stirring occasionally.

HARD SAUCE

Beat ½ cup margarine or butter, softened, in small mixer bowl on high speed until smooth, about 5 minutes. Gradually beat in 1 cup powdered sugar and 2 teaspoons vanilla or 1 tablespoon rum. Refrigerate 1 hour.

Cranberry-Angel Trifle

1 envelope (about 2 ounces)
    dessert topping mix or
    1 cup whipping cream
1 package (3¾ ounces) instant
    vanilla pudding and pie
    filling
1 teaspoon almond extract

½ white angel food cake, torn
    into 1-inch pieces
    (8 to 10 cups)
1 jar (14 ounces) cranberry-
    orange relish
    Toasted Slivered Almonds
    (below)

Prepare dessert topping mix as directed on package or beat whipping cream in chilled bowl until stiff. Prepare pudding and pie filling as directed on package. Fold whipped topping and almond extract into pudding. Alternate 3 layers each of cake pieces, cranberry-orange relish and pudding mixture in 3-quart serving bowl or casserole. Sprinkle with toasted almonds. Refrigerate at least 5 hours. *12 to 15 servings*.

TOASTED SLIVERED ALMONDS

Heat oven to 350°. Place 2 to 3 tablespoons slivered almonds in shallow baking pan. Bake until light brown, about 5 minutes.

Raspberry Trifle

½ cup sugar
3 tablespoons cornstarch
¼ teaspoon salt
3 cups milk
½ cup dry white wine*
3 egg yolks, beaten
3 tablespoons margarine or butter
1 tablespoon vanilla

2 packages (3 ounces each) ladyfingers
½ cup raspberry preserves
1 package (12 ounces) frozen raspberries, thawed
1 cup whipping cream
2 tablespoons sugar
2 tablespoons toasted slivered almonds

Mix ½ cup sugar, the cornstarch and salt in 3-quart saucepan; gradually stir in milk and wine. Heat to boiling over medium heat, stirring constantly. Boil and stir 1 minute. Stir at least half of the hot mixture gradually into egg yolks. Blend into hot mixture in saucepan. Boil and stir 1 minute. Remove from heat; stir in margarine and vanilla. Cover and refrigerate at least 3 hours.

Split ladyfingers lengthwise into halves; spread each half with raspberry preserves. Layer ¼ of the ladyfingers, cut sides up, half of the raspberries and half of the pudding in 2-quart serving bowl; repeat. Arrange remaining ladyfingers around edge of bowl in upright position with cut sides toward center. (It may be necessary to gently ease ladyfingers down into pudding about 1 inch so they remain upright.) Cover and refrigerate.

Beat whipping cream and 2 tablespoons sugar in chilled bowl until stiff; spread over dessert. Sprinkle with almonds. *8 to 10 servings.*

*⅓ cup orange juice and 2 tablespoons sherry flavoring can be substituted for the wine.

Of the many sweet puddings from the British Isles, this elaborate concoction—oddly enough, called a "trifle"!—is a very popular holiday dessert.

Cherry Layer Dessert

30 graham cracker squares
1 cup dairy sour cream or unflavored yogurt
2 cups milk
1 package (about 6 ounces) vanilla instant pudding and pie filling

1 can (21 ounces) cherry pie filling

Arrange half of the crackers in ungreased baking pan, 13x9x2 inches. Beat sour cream and milk with hand beater until smooth. Add instant pudding; beat until smooth and slightly thickened, about 2 minutes. Spread half of the pudding mixture over crackers. Add remaining crackers; spread with remaining pudding mixture. Top with pie filling. Cover and refrigerate at least 3 hours. Cut into squares. *12 to 15 servings.*

Rice appears in many Christmas menus throughout the world. In Puerto Rico, coconut rice pudding is the traditional Christmas-day dessert. In some Scandinavian homes, a bowl of rice porridge is placed in the attic for the Christmas elves.

Rice Pudding with Raspberry Sauce

⅔ cup sugar
½ cup water
2 envelopes unflavored
   gelatin
½ teaspoon salt

2 cups milk
1½ cups cooked rice
2 teaspoons vanilla
1 cup whipping cream
Raspberry Sauce (below)

Heat sugar, water, gelatin and salt in 2-quart saucepan, stirring constantly, until gelatin is dissolved, about 1 minute. Stir in milk, rice and vanilla. Place saucepan in bowl of iced water, stirring occasionally, until mixture mounds slightly when dropped from a spoon, about 10 minutes.

Beat whipping cream in chilled bowl until stiff. Fold whipped cream into rice mixture. Pour into ungreased 6-cup mold or serving bowl. Cover and refrigerate until firm, about 3 hours. Unmold by dipping briefly in warm water and loosening edge with spatula; invert on serving plate. Serve with Raspberry Sauce. *8 servings.*

RASPBERRY SAUCE
1 package (10 ounces) frozen
   raspberries, thawed

1 tablespoon cold water
2 teaspoons cornstarch

Heat raspberries (with syrup) to boiling. Mix water and cornstarch; stir into raspberries. Heat to boiling, stirring constantly. Boil and stir 1 minute. Cool. Press through a sieve to remove seeds.

☐ **Microwave Tip:** Mix all ingredients for Raspberry Sauce in 4-cup glass measure. Microwave uncovered on high (100%), stirring every minute until mixture thickens and boils, 4 to 5 minutes.

Pasta-Raisin Pudding

7 ounces uncooked vermicelli
2 packages (8 ounces each)
   cream cheese, softened
¾ cup sugar
3 eggs
2 teaspoons vanilla
¼ teaspoon salt

1 carton (16 ounces) dairy
   sour cream (2 cups)
1½ cups golden raisins
Ground nutmeg
Cranberry Topping
   (page 61)

Heat oven to 375°. Cook vermicelli as directed on package; drain. Beat cream cheese, sugar, eggs, vanilla and salt in large mixer bowl until light and fluffy; fold in sour cream, vermicelli and raisins. Pour into greased baking dish, 13x9x2 inches; sprinkle with nutmeg. Bake until brown around edges, about 45 minutes. Serve with Cranberry Topping. Garnish with whipped cream if desired. *12 servings.*

Pineapple-Banana Dessert

2½ cups graham cracker
    crumbs (about
    32 squares)
½ cup margarine or butter,
    melted
1½ cups powdered sugar
½ cup margarine or butter,
    softened
1 tablespoon hot water

1 teaspoon vanilla
3 or 4 bananas, sliced (about
    2 cups)
1 can (20 ounces) crushed
    pineapple, well drained
1 carton (8 ounces) dessert
    topping, thawed (about
    3½ cups)
12 to 15 maraschino cherries

Mix cracker crumbs and melted margarine; reserve ½ cup for topping. Press remaining crumb mixture firmly in ungreased baking pan, 13x9x2 inches. Beat powdered sugar, softened margarine, hot water and vanilla in small mixer bowl on high speed until light and fluffy, about 1 minute. Carefully spread over crumb mixture. Arrange bananas on top; spoon pineapple over bananas. Spread dessert topping over pineapple. Sprinkle with reserved crumb mixture. Cover and refrigerate at least 3 hours. Cut into squares; top each with maraschino cherry.   *12 to 15 servings.*

Cranberry Cheesecake

1¼ cups graham cracker
    crumbs (about
    16 squares)
2 tablespoons sugar
¼ cup margarine or butter,
    melted
2 packages (8 ounces each)
    cream cheese, softened
2 eggs

¾ cup sugar
2 teaspoons vanilla
1 carton (8 ounces) dairy
    sour cream (1 cup)
2 tablespoons sugar
2 teaspoons vanilla
    Cranberry Topping (below)
    or sweetened sliced
    strawberries

Heat oven to 350°. Mix cracker crumbs and 2 tablespoons sugar; stir in margarine. Press in ungreased baking pan, 9x9x2 inches, or against bottom and side of 9-inch pie plate. Beat cream cheese slightly. Add eggs, ¾ cup sugar and 2 teaspoons vanilla; beat until light and fluffy. Pour over crumb mixture.

Bake until firm, about 25 minutes. Mix sour cream, 2 tablespoons sugar and 2 teaspoons vanilla; spread carefully over warm cheesecake. Cool. Refrigerate at least 3 hours. Spoon Cranberry Topping over each serving.   *9 to 12 servings.*

CRANBERRY TOPPING
Heat ¾ cup sugar and ½ cup corn syrup to boiling. Add 2 cups cranberries; heat to boiling. Simmer 1 minute; remove from heat. Cool.

Cranberry Cheesecake

Lime Yogurt Dessert

1 cup boiling water
1 package (3 ounces) lime
   flavored gelatin

4 to 6 ice cubes
1 carton (8 ounces) lime
   flavored yogurt (1 cup)

Pour boiling water over gelatin in large bowl; stir until gelatin is dissolved. Add ice cubes; stir until gelatin begins to thicken. Remove any remaining unmelted ice.

Add yogurt; beat with hand beater until smooth. Pour into dessert dishes or parfait glasses. Refrigerate until firm, about 45 minutes. Serve with dollop of whipped cream on each and top with maraschino cherry if desired. *5 or 6 servings.*

Angel Meringue Torte

6 egg whites
½ teaspoon cream of tartar
¼ teaspoon salt
1½ cups sugar
½ teaspoon vanilla
½ teaspoon almond extract

1 cup whipping cream
Cranberries Jubilee
   (below), Cranberry
   Topping (page 61) or
   sweetened sliced
   strawberries

Heat oven to 450°. Butter bottom only of 9-inch springform pan or tube pan, 10x4 inches. Beat egg whites, cream of tartar and salt in large mixer bowl on medium speed until foamy. On high speed, beat in sugar, 2 tablespoons at a time; beat until stiff and glossy. Beat in vanilla and almond extract. Do not underbeat. Spread evenly in pan. Place in oven; immediately turn off oven. Leave pan in oven at least 8 hours.

Run knife around torte to loosen; invert on serving plate. Beat whipping cream in chilled bowl until stiff. Frost torte with whipped cream. Refrigerate at least 4 hours. Cut into wedges and serve with Cranberries Jubilee. *12 servings.*

CRANBERRIES JUBILEE
¾ teaspoon grated orange peel
½ cup orange juice
½ cup water
2 cups sugar

2 cups cranberries
2 tablespoons water
2 teaspoons cornstarch
¼ cup brandy

Mix orange peel, orange juice, ½ cup water and the sugar in 2-quart saucepan. Heat to boiling; boil 5 minutes. Stir in cranberries. Heat to boiling; boil rapidly 5 minutes. Mix 2 tablespoons water and the cornstarch; stir into cranberry mixture. Cook, stirring constantly, until mixture thickens and boils. Boil and stir 1 minute.

Pour cranberry mixture into chafing dish to keep warm. Heat brandy in saucepan until warm; ignite and pour over cranberry mixture.

Cherry-Berries on a Cloud

6 egg whites	1 teaspoon vanilla
½ teaspoon cream of tartar	2 cups whipping cream
1½ cups sugar	2 cups miniature
2 packages (3 ounces each)	marshmallows
cream cheese, softened	Cherry-Berry Topping
½ cup sugar	(below)

Heat oven to 275°. Grease baking pan, 13x9x2 inches. Beat egg whites and cream of tartar in large mixer bowl on medium speed until foamy. On high speed, beat in 1½ cups sugar, 1 tablespoon at a time; beat until stiff and glossy. Do not underbeat. Spread in pan. Bake 1 hour. Turn off oven; leave in oven with door closed at least 12 hours.

Mix cream cheese, ½ cup sugar and the vanilla. Beat whipping cream in chilled bowl until stiff. Fold whipped cream and marshmallows into cream cheese mixture; spread over meringue. Refrigerate at least 6 hours. Cut into serving pieces and top with Cherry-Berry Topping. *12 to 15 servings.*

CHERRY-BERRY TOPPING
Mix 1 can (21 ounces) cherry pie filling, 2 cups sliced strawberries or 1 package (16 ounces) frozen strawberries (thawed) and 1 teaspoon lemon juice.

Lime Meringue Dessert

6 egg whites	½ cup lime juice (3 or 4 limes)
½ teaspoon cream of tartar	3 or 4 drops green food color
1½ cups sugar	1½ cups whipping cream
6 egg yolks	1 to 1½ tablespoons grated
¾ cup sugar	lime peel
¼ teaspoon salt	

Heat oven to 275°. Grease baking pan, 13x9x2 inches. Beat egg whites and cream of tartar in large mixer bowl on medium speed until foamy. On high speed, beat in 1½ cups sugar, 1 tablespoon at a time; beat until stiff and glossy. Do not underbeat. Spread in pan. Bake 1 hour. Turn off oven; leave in oven with door closed at least 12 hours.

Beat egg yolks in small mixer bowl until light and lemon colored. Mix egg yolks, ¾ cup sugar, the salt and lime juice in saucepan. Cook over medium heat, stirring constantly, until mixture thickens, about 5 minutes. Cool to room temperature; stir in food color. Beat whipping cream in chilled bowl until stiff. Fold whipped cream and lime peel into lime mixture; spread over meringue. Refrigerate at least 4 hours. Cut into squares. Garnish each with lime twist if desired. *12 to 15 servings.*

Note: Dessert can be tightly covered and frozen no longer than 3 weeks. Let stand at room temperature 30 minutes before serving.

Frosty Pumpkin Squares

1¼ cups graham cracker
    crumbs (about
    16 squares)
¼ cup margarine or butter,
    melted
1 cup mashed cooked
    pumpkin

½ cup packed brown sugar
½ teaspoon salt
½ teaspoon ground cinnamon
½ teaspoon ground ginger
¼ teaspoon ground nutmeg
1 quart vanilla ice cream,
    softened

Mix cracker crumbs and margarine. Reserve 2 to 3 tablespoons crumb mixture; press remaining mixture in ungreased baking pan, 8x8x2 or 9x9x2 inches.

Beat pumpkin, brown sugar, salt and spices until well blended. Stir in ice cream. Pour into pan; sprinkle with reserved crumb mixture. Freeze until firm, about 4 hours. Remove from freezer 10 to 15 minutes before serving. *9 servings.*

Crunchy Ice-Cream Squares

2 cups coarsely crushed corn
    flake or whole wheat flake
    cereal
1 can (3½ ounces) flaked
    coconut (1⅓ cups)
½ cup chopped nuts
½ cup packed brown sugar

⅓ cup margarine or butter,
    melted
½ gallon vanilla, butter pecan,
    butterscotch revel or
    chocolate ice cream,
    softened

Mix cereal, coconut, nuts, brown sugar and margarine. Press ⅔ of the mixture (about 3½ cups) in ungreased baking pan, 13x9x2 inches. Slice ice cream; press on cereal layer. Sprinkle with remaining cereal mixture. Cover and freeze until firm, at least 12 hours. *15 servings.*

Granola Ice-Cream Squares: Substitute 2 cups granola (any flavor) for the cereal, coconut and nuts.

Christmas Tortoni

⅔ cup macaroon cookie or
    vanilla wafer crumbs
    (about 12 cookies)
¼ cup cut-up red candied
    cherries

½ cup chopped salted almonds
1 quart vanilla ice cream,
    slightly softened
Red and green candied
    cherries

Mix cookie crumbs, ¼ cup cherries and the almonds; fold into ice cream. Divide ice-cream mixture among 8 paper-lined medium muffin cups, 2½x1¼ inches. Arrange red cherry half and slices of green cherry on each. Freeze until firm, about 4 hours. *8 servings.*

Christmas Tortoni

Date Dream Dessert

1 package (14 ounces) date bar
   mix
2 tablespoons margarine or
   butter, softened
¼ cup chopped nuts, if desired
½ cup hot water

1 cup whipping cream
2 tablespoons powdered sugar
1 teaspoon instant coffee
   crystals or 1 teaspoon
   vanilla

Heat oven to 400°. Mix crumb mix and margarine with fork; stir in nuts. Spread in ungreased baking pan, 13x9x2 inches. Bake 10 minutes. Stir and cool; crumble. Mix date filling and hot water; cool. Beat whipping cream, powdered sugar and coffee crystals until stiff.

Line loaf pan, 9x5x3 inches, with aluminum foil. Spread 1 cup of the crumbly mixture in pan. Spread half of the whipped cream mixture over crumbly mixture. Continue layering the following: ½ cup crumbly mixture, the date filling, ½ cup crumbly mixture, remaining whipped cream and crumbly mixture; press lightly. Freeze until firm, at least 4 hours. Remove from freezer 10 to 15 minutes before serving. *6 to 8 servings.*

Coconut Snowballs

Spread 2 cups flaked coconut in shallow pan or on plate. Place paper or foil liners in each of 12 medium muffin cups, 2½x1¼ inches. Scoop ½ gallon any flavor ice cream into 12 balls; roll each in coconut, using 2 forks for rolling. Place balls in muffin cups. Freeze until firm. Cover and freeze no longer than 2 weeks. *12 servings.*

Tinted Coconut Snowballs: Shake coconut and 4 drops red or green food color in tightly covered jar until coconut is evenly tinted. Continue as directed.

Lemon-Raspberry Parfaits

1 tablespoon sugar
2 teaspoons cornstarch
2 tablespoons orange juice
1 package (10 ounces) frozen
   raspberries, partially
   thawed

1 teaspoon grated orange peel
1 quart lemon sherbet

Mix sugar and cornstarch in 1-quart saucepan. Stir in orange juice, raspberries and orange peel. Cook over medium heat, stirring constantly, until mixture thickens and boils. Boil and stir 1 minute. Refrigerate until cool. Layer lemon sherbet and raspberry sauce in parfait glasses. Freeze until firm. Remove from freezer 10 to 15 minutes before serving. Top with whipped cream and lemon twists if desired. *6 servings.*

Lemon-Raspberry Parfaits

Pumpkin Pie

Pastry for 9-inch One-Crust
Pie (page 71)
2 eggs
1 can (16 ounces) pumpkin
¾ cup sugar
½ teaspoon salt

1 teaspoon ground
cinnamon
½ teaspoon ground ginger
¼ teaspoon ground cloves
1⅔ cups evaporated milk or
half-and-half

Heat oven to 425°. Prepare pastry. Beat eggs slightly with hand beater; beat in remaining ingredients. Place pastry-lined pie plate on oven rack; pour in filling. Bake 15 minutes.

Reduce oven temperature to 350°. Bake until knife inserted in center comes out clean, 45 minutes; cool. Serve with sweetened whipped cream if desired.

Carrot Pie: Substitute 2 cups mashed cooked carrots for the canned pumpkin.

Squash Pie: Substitute 2 cups mashed cooked winter squash for the canned pumpkin.

Sweet Potato Pie: Substitute 2 cups mashed cooked sweet potatoes for the canned pumpkin.

Apple-Mince Pie

Pastry for 9-inch One-Crust
Pie (page 71)
¼ cup all-purpose flour
⅓ cup sugar
⅛ teaspoon salt
1 tablespoon margarine or
butter

¼ cup water
2 tablespoons red cinnamon
candies
1 jar (18 ounces) prepared
mincemeat (2 cups)
3 tart apples

Heat oven to 425°. Prepare pastry. Sprinkle 2 tablespoons of the flour in pastry-lined pie plate. Mix remaining flour, the sugar, salt and margarine until crumbly. Heat water and cinnamon candies, stirring until candies are dissolved. Spread mincemeat on pastry.

Pare apples and cut into fourths; cut into wedges, ½ inch thick at outer side. Cover mincemeat with 2 circles of overlapping apple wedges; sprinkle with sugar mixture. Spoon cinnamon syrup over top, moistening as much sugar mixture as possible.

Cover edge with 2- to 3-inch strip of aluminum foil to prevent excessive browning; remove foil during last 15 minutes of baking. Bake until crust is golden brown, 40 to 50 minutes.

Chess Pie

Pastry for 9-inch One-Crust
 Pie (page 71)
3 egg yolks
⅔ cup sugar
1 tablespoon flour

½ teaspoon salt
1⅓ cups whipping cream
1 cup cut-up dates
1 cup chopped walnuts
1 teaspoon vanilla

Heat oven to 350°. Prepare pastry. Beat egg yolks, sugar, flour and salt in small mixer bowl until light and lemon colored. Stir in whipping cream, dates, walnuts and vanilla. Pour into pastry-lined pie plate. Bake until crust is golden brown, 50 to 60 minutes.

Old-Fashioned Mince Pie

Heat oven to 425°. Prepare pastry for 9-inch Two-Crust Pie (page 71). Mix 1 jar (28 ounces) prepared mincemeat and 1½ cups diced pared tart apples; pour into pastry-lined pie plate. Cover with top crust that has slits cut in it; seal and flute. Cover edge with 2- to 3-inch strip of aluminum foil to prevent excessive browning; remove foil during last 15 minutes of baking. Bake until crust is golden brown, 40 to 45 minutes.

Flaming Mince Pie: Prepare Old-Fashioned Mince Pie (above) except—do not cut slits in top crust. Cut out 1¼-inch circles (one for center of each serving) about ½ inch from edge of pie. Bake as directed. Curl ½-inch-wide circular strips of orange peel to resemble blossoms; place in circles. Soak sugar cubes in lemon extract about 5 minutes; insert one in each blossom and ignite.

Mincemeat pies—''Christmas pies''—have been made in England at holiday time since the Middle Ages.

Cranberry-Apple Pie

Pastry for 9-inch Two-Crust
 Pie (page 71)
1¾ to 2 cups sugar
¼ cup all-purpose flour
3 cups sliced pared tart
 apples (about 3 medium)

2 cups fresh or thawed frozen
 cranberries
2 tablespoons margarine or
 butter

Heat oven to 425°. Prepare pastry. Mix sugar and flour. Alternate layers of apples, cranberries and sugar mixture in pastry-lined pie plate, beginning and ending with apples. Dot with margarine. Cover with top crust that has slits cut in it; seal and flute. Cover edge with 2- to 3-inch strip of aluminum foil to prevent excessive browning; remove foil during last 15 minutes of baking.

Bake until crust is brown and juice begins to bubble through slits in crust, 40 to 50 minutes. Serve with ice cream if desired.

Partridge in a Pear Tree Pie

3 cups (12 ounces)
    cranberries
1½ cups sugar
1 can (8¾ ounces) crushed
    pineapple, drained
    (reserve syrup)
    Pastry for 9-inch Two-Crust
    Pie (page 71)

3 tablespoons flour
¼ teaspoon salt
¼ teaspoon ground cinnamon
1 can (8 ounces) pear halves,
    drained and cut into
    halves
    Sugar

Cook cranberries, 1½ cups sugar, the pineapple and ¼ cup of the reserved syrup, stirring constantly, until cranberries are tender, about 5 minutes. Cool. Prepare pastry as directed except—flute bottom crust. Mix flour, salt and cinnamon; stir into cranberry mixture. Pour into pastry-lined pie plate. Gently press pear slices spoke-fashion onto cranberry mixture.

Heat oven to 400°. After rolling pastry for top crust, cut partridge, leaf and pear shapes (see photograph). Sprinkle with sugar if desired; place on ungreased cookie sheet. Bake pastry cutouts and pie until cutouts and pie crust are golden brown, 7 to 10 minutes for cutouts and about 40 minutes for pie. Arrange cutouts on pie.

You can fashion other pastry cutouts for your Christmas pies: Use a cookie cutter (bell, star, tree) or cut around your own patterns. For an unusual and colorful finish, decorate the unbaked cutouts with Egg Yolk Paint (page 12).

Della Robbia Apple Pie

    Pastry for 9-inch Two-Crust
    Pie (page 71)
4 cups diced pared tart apples
¼ cup lemon juice
½ cup cut-up dates
½ cup maraschino cherries, cut
    into fourths

½ cup coarsely chopped
    walnuts
½ cup sugar
¼ cup all-purpose flour
¼ teaspoon salt
¼ cup half-and-half
    Della Robbia Wreath (below)

Heat oven to 425°. Prepare pastry. Mix apples and lemon juice. Stir in remaining ingredients except Della Robbia Wreath. Pour into pastry-lined pie plate. Cover with top crust that has slits cut in it; seal and flute. Cover edge with 2- to 3-inch strip of aluminum foil to prevent excessive browning; remove foil during last 15 minutes of baking. Bake until crust is brown and juice begins to bubble through slits in crust, 50 to 60 minutes. Cool. Garnish with wreath.

DELLA ROBBIA WREATH
Mold process cheese into small apple and pear shapes; sprinkle tops with red sugar. Arrange cheese fruits, green and red maraschino cherries and dates in the shape of a wreath on pie.

Opposite: On the first day of Christmas . . . a Partridge in a Pear Tree Pie

Peppermint Stick Pie

Chocolate Cookie Crust
(below)
24 large marshmallows
½ cup milk
1 teaspoon vanilla
⅛ teaspoon salt

6 drops peppermint extract
6 drops red food color
1 cup whipping cream
2 tablespoons crushed
peppermint candy

Bake Chocolate Cookie Crust. Heat marshmallows and milk over low heat, stirring constantly, just until marshmallows are melted. Remove from heat; stir in vanilla, salt, peppermint extract and food color. Refrigerate, stirring occasionally, until mixture mounds slightly when dropped from a spoon.

Beat whipping cream in chilled bowl until stiff. Stir marshmallow mixture until blended; fold into whipped cream. Pour into crust. Refrigerate at least 12 hours. Just before serving, sprinkle with crushed candy.

CHOCOLATE COOKIE CRUST

Heat oven to 350°. Mix 1½ cups chocolate wafer crumbs and ¼ cup margarine or butter, melted. Press firmly against bottom and side of ungreased 9-inch pie plate. Bake 10 minutes. Cool.

Grasshopper Pie

Chocolate Cookie Crust
(above)
32 large marshmallows
½ cup milk
¼ cup crème de menthe

3 tablespoons white crème
de cacao
1½ cups whipping cream
Few drops green food
color, if desired

Bake Chocolate Cookie Crust. Heat marshmallows and milk over medium heat, stirring constantly, just until marshmallows are melted. Refrigerate until thickened; stir in liqueurs.

Beat whipping cream in chilled bowl until stiff. Fold marshmallow mixture into whipped cream; fold in food color. Pour into crust. Sprinkle with grated semisweet chocolate if desired. Refrigerate until set, at least 3 hours.

Grasshopper Tarts: Omit Chocolate Cookie Crust. Heat 1 package (12 ounces) semisweet chocolate chips and 2 tablespoons shortening over medium heat, stirring constantly, until chocolate is melted, 3 to 4 minutes. Line 12 medium muffin cups, 2½x1¼ inches, with paper baking cups. Swirl 1 tablespoon chocolate mixture in each cup with back of spoon to coat bottom and side. Refrigerate until firm. Fill in with remaining chocolate. Refrigerate until firm. Carefully remove paper baking cups from chocolate shells. Return shells to muffin cups. Divide filling for Grasshopper Pie (above) among shells. Refrigerate until set, 2 to 3 hours. Garnish with whipped cream if desired. *12 servings.*

Grasshopper Tarts

Pastry

8- OR 9-INCH ONE-CRUST PIE

⅓ cup plus 1 tablespoon
    shortening or ⅓ cup lard
1 cup all-purpose flour

½ teaspoon salt*
2 to 3 tablespoons cold water

8- OR 9-INCH TWO-CRUST PIE

⅔ cup plus 2 tablespoons
    shortening or ⅔ cup lard
2 cups all-purpose flour

1 teaspoon salt*
4 to 5 tablespoons cold water

Cut shortening into flour and salt until particles are size of small peas. Sprinkle in water, 1 tablespoon at a time, tossing with fork until all flour is moistened and pastry almost cleans side of bowl (1 to 2 teaspoons water can be added if necessary).

Gather pastry into a ball; shape into flattened round on lightly floured cloth-covered board. (For Two-Crust Pie, divide pastry into halves and shape into 2 rounds.) Roll pastry 2 inches larger than inverted pie plate with floured stockinet-covered rolling pin. Fold pastry into quarters; unfold and ease into plate, pressing firmly against bottom and side.

For One-Crust Pie: Trim overhanging edge of pastry 1 inch from rim of plate. Fold and roll pastry under, even with plate; flute. Fill and bake as directed in recipe.

For Baked Pie Shell: Prick bottom and side thoroughly with fork. Bake at 475° until light brown, 8 to 10 minutes; cool.

For Two-Crust Pie: Turn desired filling into pastry-lined pie plate. Trim overhanging edge of pastry ½ inch from rim of plate. Roll other round of pastry. Fold into quarters; cut slits so steam can escape. Place over filling and unfold. Trim overhanging edge of pastry 1 inch from rim of plate. Fold and roll top edge under lower edge, pressing on rim to seal; flute. Cover edge with 2- to 3-inch strip of aluminum foil to prevent excessive browning; remove foil during last 15 minutes of baking. Bake as directed in recipe.

*If using self-rising flour, omit salt. Pie crusts made with self-rising or whole wheat flour differ in flavor and texture from those made with all-purpose flour.

Note: If possible, hook fluted edge over edge of pie plate to prevent shrinking and help pastry retain its shape.

Whole Wheat Pastry: Prepare filling before preparing pastry. Substitute whole wheat flour for the all-purpose flour or substitute stone-ground whole wheat flour for half of the all-purpose flour. Fold rolled pastry in half instead of into quarters.

Holiday Pastry Snacks: Heat oven to 475°. Gather leftover rolled pastry into a ball; shape into flattened round. Roll ⅛ inch thick. Cut into desired shapes with Christmas cookie cutters. Prick and sprinkle with colored sugars, cinnamon-sugar and/or finely chopped nuts. Place on ungreased cookie sheet; bake 8 to 10 minutes.

Cream Puffs

1 cup water	4 eggs
½ cup margarine or butter	Fillings (below)
1 cup all-purpose flour	

Heat oven to 400°. Heat water and margarine to rolling boil in 1-quart saucepan. Stir in flour. Stir vigorously over low heat until mixture forms a ball, about 1 minute. Remove from heat. Add eggs; beat until smooth. Drop dough by scant ¼ cupfuls 3 inches apart onto ungreased cookie sheet.

Bake until puffed and golden, 35 to 40 minutes. Cool. Cut off tops of puffs; pull out any filaments of soft dough. Fill puffs with one of the Fillings; replace tops.   *10 to 12 cream puffs.*

EGGNOG FLUFF FILLING

1 package (3¾ ounces) vanilla instant pudding and pie filling	1 teaspoon ground nutmeg
	¼ teaspoon ground ginger
1 cup milk	2 cups whipping cream
1 teaspoon rum flavoring	Powdered sugar

Blend pudding and pie filling, milk, rum flavoring, nutmeg and ginger in large mixer bowl on low speed. Add whipping cream; beat on high speed until soft peaks form, 1 to 2 minutes. Fill puffs. Serve immediately or cover and refrigerate no longer than 3 hours. Just before serving, sprinkle with powdered sugar or brush tops with light corn syrup and sprinkle with nonpareils.

ICE-CREAM FILLING

Fill cooled puffs with peppermint, pistachio or vanilla ice cream. Serve immediately or cover and freeze no longer than 24 hours; let stand a few minutes at room temperature before serving. Serve with Hot Fudge Sauce (page 163) or sprinkle with powdered sugar.

PEPPERMINT WHIPPED CREAM FILLING

Beat 2 cups whipping cream, ¼ cup granulated or powdered sugar, 1 teaspoon peppermint extract and 5 or 6 drops red or green food color in chilled bowl until stiff. Fill puffs. Serve immediately or cover and refrigerate no longer than 4 hours. Serve with Hot Fudge Sauce (page 163).

Note: To freeze unbaked cream puff dough, place mounds of dough in freezer, uncovered. Freeze until firm, about 4 hours. Store in freezer bags in freezer no longer than 1 month. To bake, heat oven to 400°. Bake frozen puffs 3 inches apart on ungreased cookie sheet. Bake until puffed and golden, 45 to 50 minutes. To freeze baked puffs, wrap, label and freeze no longer than 3 months. Thaw unwrapped at room temperature about 30 minutes.

Cream Puffs

Cardamom Cream Crepes

Crepes (below)
¾ cup whipping cream
¼ cup packed brown sugar
¼ teaspoon ground cardamom

⅓ cup dairy sour cream
1 jar (14 ounces) cranberry
   sauce or lingonberries

Prepare Crepes. Beat whipping cream, brown sugar and cardamom in chilled bowl just until soft peaks form, about 2 minutes. Fold in sour cream. Spoon about 2 tablespoons cream mixture onto each crepe; roll up. Place 2 crepes seam sides down on each dessert plate. Top with cranberry sauce.   *8 servings (2 crepes each).*

CREPES

1½ cups all-purpose flour
 1 tablespoon sugar
 ½ teaspoon baking powder
 ½ teaspoon salt
 2 cups milk

2 eggs
2 tablespoons margarine or
   butter, melted
½ teaspoon vanilla

Mix flour, sugar, baking powder and salt. Stir in remaining ingredients. Beat with hand beater until smooth. Lightly butter 6-inch skillet; heat over medium heat until bubbly. Pour scant ¼ cup of the batter into skillet; immediately rotate skillet until thin film covers bottom.

Cook until light brown. Run wide spatula around edge to loosen; turn and cook other side until light brown. Stack crepes, placing waxed paper between each. Keep covered.   *16 crepes.*

Note: Crepes may be made ahead of time, then refrigerated or frozen. Stack 6 to 8 together, with a layer of waxed paper between each. Wrap and refrigerate for several days. For long-term storage, wrap, label and freeze. When ready to use, thaw (wrapped) at room temperature about 3 hours. Crepes freeze well but should be stored in the freezer no longer than 3 months.

Raspberry-Almond Crepes

Crepes (above)
1 package (3¾ ounces) vanilla
   instant pudding and pie
   filling
2 cups half-and-half

½ teaspoon almond extract
1 tablespoon cornstarch
1 package (10 ounces) frozen
   raspberries, thawed
   Sliced almonds

Prepare Crepes. Prepare pudding and pie filling as directed on package except—substitute half-and-half for the milk and beat in almond extract. Refrigerate at least 30 minutes.

Place cornstarch in 1-quart saucepan; gradually stir in raspberries. Cook over low heat, stirring constantly, until mixture thickens and boils. Boil and stir 1 minute; cool. Spoon about 2 tablespoons pudding mixture onto each crepe; roll up. Place 2 crepes seam sides down on each dessert plate. Top with raspberry sauce and sprinkle with sliced almonds.   *8 servings (2 crepes each).*

Raspberry-Almond Crepes

Breads

The timeless pleasures of breadmaking are most rewarding in the Christmas season. Festive, fruit-studded coffee cakes . . . plump yeasty breads from the "old country" . . . fragrant nut breads . . . sweet frosted rolls and cinnamon-scented muffins: Not only will they brighten all your holiday gatherings, but many are perfect for placing—wrapped and beribboned—beneath someone's tree.

Candy Cane Coffee Cake

Candy Cane Coffee Cakes

2 packages active dry yeast	2 teaspoons baking powder
½ cup warm water (105 to 115°)	2 teaspoons salt
1¼ cups buttermilk	5½ to 6 cups all-purpose flour
½ cup sugar	1½ cups snipped dried apricots
½ cup margarine or butter, softened	1½ cups chopped drained maraschino cherries
2 eggs	Glaze (below)

Dissolve yeast in warm water in large mixer bowl. Add buttermilk, sugar, margarine, eggs, baking powder, salt and 2½ cups of the flour. Beat on low speed, scraping bowl constantly, 30 seconds. Beat on medium speed, scraping bowl occasionally, 2 minutes. Stir in enough remaining flour to make dough easy to handle. (Dough will be soft and slightly sticky.)

Turn dough onto well-floured surface; knead until smooth and elastic, about 5 minutes. Divide into 3 equal parts. Roll each part into rectangle, 15x6 inches. Place on greased cookie sheet. Make 2-inch cuts on 15-inch sides of rectangles at ½-inch intervals. Mix apricots and cherries.

Spread ⅓ of the fruit mixture lengthwise down center of each rectangle. Crisscross strips over fruit mixture. Stretch each rectangle to 22 inches; curve to form cane. Cover; let rise in warm place until double, about 1 hour. (Dough is ready if indentation remains when touched.)

Heat oven 375°. Bake until golden brown, 18 to 20 minutes. Drizzle Glaze over canes while warm. Decorate with cherry halves or pieces if desired.   *3 coffee cakes.*

GLAZE
Mix 2 cups powdered sugar and about 2 tablespoons water until smooth and of desired consistency.

Saint Lucia Crown

¹⁄₁₆ to ⅛ teaspoon crushed
    saffron*
½ cup lukewarm milk
    (scalded then cooled)
2 packages active dry yeast
½ cup warm water
    (105 to 115°)
½ cup sugar
1 teaspoon salt
2 eggs, beaten
¼ cup margarine or butter,
    softened

4½ to 5 cups all-purpose flour
½ cup cut-up citron
¼ cup chopped blanched
    almonds
1 tablespoon grated lemon
    peel
    Powdered Sugar Glaze
    (below)
    Candied cherries

Stir saffron into milk. Dissolve yeast in warm water in large bowl. Stir in saffron-milk, sugar, salt, eggs, margarine and 2½ cups of the flour. Beat until smooth. Stir in citron, almonds, lemon peel and enough remaining flour to make dough easy to handle.

Turn dough onto lightly floured surface; knead until smooth and elastic, about 10 minutes. Place in greased bowl; turn greased side up. Cover; let rise in warm place until double, about 1½ hours. (Dough is ready if indentation remains when touched.)

Punch down dough; cut off ⅓ of the dough for top braid and reserve. Divide remaining dough into 3 equal parts; roll each part into 25-inch strip. Place close together on greased cookie sheet. Braid strips; shape into circle and pinch ends to seal.

Divide reserved dough into 3 equal parts; roll each part into 16-inch strip. Place close together on another greased cookie sheet. Braid strips; shape into circle and pinch ends to seal. Cover both braids; let rise until double, about 45 minutes.

Heat oven to 375°. Bake until golden brown, 20 to 25 minutes. When cool, make holes for 5 candles in small braid. Drizzle both braids with Powdered Sugar Glaze; garnish with cherries. Insert candles. Place small braid on large braid.

*2 or 3 drops of yellow food color can be substituted for the saffron.

POWDERED SUGAR GLAZE
Mix 1 cup powdered sugar and 3 to 4 teaspoons water until smooth and of desired consistency.

Lucia Buns: When ready to shape dough, cut into pieces about 2½ inches in diameter. Shape each piece into 12-inch roll; form into tightly coiled "S" shape. Place a raisin in center of each coil. Place on greased cookie sheet. Brush tops lightly with margarine or butter; let rise until double, about 45 minutes. Bake until golden brown, about 15 minutes. *About 1½ dozen buns.*

The Christmas season begins in Sweden on Luciadagen—St. Lucia Day—named for the legendary young saint who symbolizes hospitality. In Swedish homes the daughters rise early on December 13 to serve their parents coffee and the traditional saffron buns.

Lucia Buns

Fruited Christmas Wreath

2 packages active dry yeast	2 teaspoons salt
½ cup warm water (105 to 115°)	5½ cups all-purpose flour
	1 cup cut-up mixed candied fruit
1¼ cups buttermilk	
½ cup granulated sugar	½ cup chopped pecans
½ cup margarine or butter, softened	1 tablespoon grated lemon peel
2 eggs	½ cup powdered sugar
2 teaspoons baking powder	1 tablespoon milk

Dissolve yeast in warm water in large mixer bowl. Add buttermilk, granulated sugar, margarine, eggs, baking powder, salt and 2½ cups of the flour. Beat on low speed, scraping bowl constantly, 30 seconds. Beat on medium speed, scraping bowl occasionally, 2 minutes. Stir in remaining flour, the candied fruit, pecans and lemon peel. (Dough will be soft and slightly sticky.)

Turn dough onto well-floured surface; knead until smooth and elastic, about 5 minutes. Roll into strip, 24x6 inches. Cut into 3 strips, 24x2 inches. Place close together on greased cookie sheet. Braid strips; shape into circle and pinch ends to seal. Cover; let rise in warm place until double, about 1 hour. (Dough is ready if indentation remains when touched.)

Heat oven to 375°. Bake until golden brown, about 30 minutes. Mix powdered sugar and milk; drizzle over wreath while warm. Decorate with green and red candied cherries if desired. *1 large coffee cake.*

Note: For two small wreaths, divide dough after kneading into halves. Roll each half into rectangle, 18x3 inches. Cut into 3 strips, each 18x1 inch. Continue as directed except—bake 20 to 30 minutes. Omit powdered sugar and milk and brush with softened margarine or butter if desired.

Christmas Tree Bread: Omit candied fruit, pecans, lemon peel, powdered sugar and milk. Divide dough into halves; shape 1 half at a time into seventeen 2-inch balls. Form tree shape with balls in rows of 5, 4, 3, 2, 1 on lightly greased cookie sheet. Roll remaining 2 balls together for trunk of tree. Cover; let rise in warm place 1 hour. Bake until golden brown, 20 to 25 minutes. Remove from cookie sheets and cool.

Beat 2 cups powdered sugar, 2 to 3 tablespoons water or milk and 1 teaspoon vanilla until smooth. Decorate trees with frosting. Trim with candied fruits. *2 coffee cakes.*

Opposite: Christmas Tree Bread

One of Scandinavia's most popular Christmas coffee cakes.

Julekage

1 package active dry yeast	1 egg
¼ cup warm water (105 to 115°)	2 tablespoons shortening
¾ cup lukewarm milk (scalded then cooled)	½ cup raisins
½ cup sugar	⅓ cup cut-up citron
½ teaspoon salt	3¼ to 3¾ cups all-purpose flour
½ teaspoon ground cardamom	Egg Yolk Glaze (below)

Dissolve yeast in warm water in large bowl. Beat in milk, sugar, salt, cardamom, egg, shortening, raisins, citron and 1½ cups of the flour. Beat until smooth. Stir in enough remaining flour to make dough easy to handle.

Turn dough onto lightly floured surface; knead until smooth and elastic, about 5 minutes. Place in greased bowl; turn greased side up. Cover; let rise in warm place until double, about 1½ hours. (Dough is ready if indentation remains when touched.)

Punch down dough; shape into round loaf. Place in greased round layer pan, 9x1½ inches. Cover; let rise until double, about 45 minutes. Heat oven to 350°. Brush dough with Egg Yolk Glaze. Bake until golden brown, 30 to 40 minutes.

EGG YOLK GLAZE
Beat 1 egg yolk and 2 tablespoons water.

Honey Crescent Rings

1 package active dry yeast	1 teaspoon salt
½ cup warm water (105 to 115°)	1 egg
½ cup lukewarm milk (scalded then cooled)	3½ to 4 cups all-purpose flour Topping (page 79)
⅓ cup sugar	¼ cup margarine or butter, softened
⅓ cup shortening, or margarine or butter, softened	½ cup sugar
	2 teaspoons ground cinnamon

Dissolve yeast in warm water in large bowl. Stir in milk, sugar, shortening, salt, egg and 2 cups of the flour. Beat until smooth. Stir in enough remaining flour to make dough easy to handle.

Turn dough onto lightly floured surface; knead until smooth and elastic, about 5 minutes. Place in greased bowl; turn greased side up. Cover; let rise in warm place until double, about 1½ hours. (Dough is ready if indentation remains when touched.)

Prepare Topping; cool slightly. Punch down dough. Divide into 3 equal parts. Roll each part into 10-inch circle on lightly floured surface. Spread about 1 tablespoon margarine and 2 tablespoons Topping over each circle. Mix sugar and cinnamon; sprinkle each circle with about 3 tablespoons mixture. Cut each circle into 12 wedges. Roll up tightly, beginning at rounded sides. Place rolls with points underneath in spoke fashion in 3 greased round layer pans, 8 or 9x1½ inches; curve slightly. Let rise in warm place until double, about 45 minutes.

Heat oven to 400°. Bake 10 minutes; spread with remaining Topping. Bake until golden brown, about 10 minutes longer. Immediately remove from pans. *3 coffee cakes.*

TOPPING

⅓ cup sugar
¼ cup finely chopped nuts
¼ cup honey

3 tablespoons margarine or
    butter
⅛ teaspoon ground cinnamon

Heat all ingredients to boiling, stirring frequently.

Christmas Tree Coffee Cakes

2 packages active dry yeast
¾ cup warm water
    (105 to 115°)
¾ cup buttermilk
¾ cup dairy sour cream
½ cup shortening
¼ cup sugar
2 teaspoons baking powder
2 teaspoons salt

5 to 5½ cups all-purpose
    flour
1½ cups cut-up candied fruit
    Margarine or butter,
    softened
    Powdered Sugar Frosting
    (below)
    Candied cherries, cut into
    halves

Dissolve yeast in warm water in large mixer bowl. Add buttermilk, sour cream, shortening, sugar, baking powder, salt and 2½ cups of the flour. Beat on low speed, scraping bowl constantly, 30 seconds. Beat on medium speed, scraping bowl occasionally, 2 minutes. Stir in candied fruit and enough remaining flour to make dough easy to handle.

Turn dough onto lightly floured surface; knead until smooth and elastic, about 5 minutes. Divide dough into 4 equal parts. Shape each part into a rope, 22 to 24 inches. Pinch off 1-inch piece for tree trunk. Shape 2 ropes into a tree, 9 inches wide at base, 11½ inches high, with 1-inch space between each row on greased cookie sheet (see diagram). Pinch to join ropes. Place 1-inch piece at base of tree. Brush with margarine. Repeat. Cover; let rise in warm place until double, about 1 hour. (Dough is ready if indentation remains when touched.) Heat oven to 375°. Bake until golden brown, 20 to 25 minutes. Cool.

Drizzle coffee cakes with Powdered Sugar Frosting. Decorate with cherry halves. *2 coffee cakes.*

POWDERED SUGAR FROSTING

Mix 2 cups powdered sugar and 2 to 3 tablespoons milk until smooth and of desired consistency.

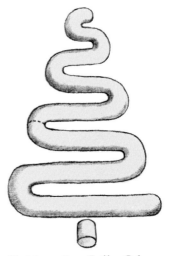

Christmas Tree Coffee Cake

Holiday Braid

1 package active dry yeast	½ cup chopped almonds
¼ cup warm water (105 to 115°)	1 teaspoon grated lemon peel
¾ cup lukewarm milk (scalded then cooled)	⅛ teaspoon ground mace
¼ cup sugar	3½ to 3¾ cups all-purpose flour
¼ cup shortening	1 egg yolk
1 teaspoon salt	2 tablespoons cold water
1 egg	Powdered Sugar Glaze (page 75)
½ cup raisins	

Dissolve yeast in warm water in large bowl. Stir in milk, sugar, shortening, salt, egg, raisins, almonds, lemon peel, mace and 1¾ cups of the flour. Beat until smooth. Stir in enough remaining flour to make dough easy to handle.

Turn dough onto lightly floured surface; knead until smooth and elastic, about 5 minutes. Place in greased bowl; turn greased side up. Cover; let rise in warm place until double, about 1½ hours. (Dough is ready if indentation remains when touched.)

Punch down dough. Divide into 4 equal parts; roll 3 of the parts into 14-inch strips. Place close together on lightly greased cookie sheet. Braid loosely; pinch ends together and fold under. Divide remaining part into 3 pieces and roll each into 12-inch strip. Braid strips; place on large braid. Cover and let rise until double, 45 to 60 minutes.

Heat oven to 350°. Mix egg yolk and cold water; brush on coffee cake. Bake until golden brown, 30 to 40 minutes. Spread with Powdered Sugar Glaze while warm.

Stollen

1 package active dry yeast	¼ cup cut-up citron
¾ cup warm water (105 to 115°)	¼ cup cut-up candied cherries, if desired
½ cup sugar	¼ cup raisins
½ cup margarine or butter, softened	1 tablespoon grated lemon peel
½ teaspoon salt	Margarine or butter, softened
3 eggs	1 tablespoon water
1 egg, separated	Creamy Frosting (page 16)
3½ cups all-purpose flour	
½ cup chopped blanched almonds	

Every province of Germany has its own recipe for Weihnachtsstollen, or Christmas bread.

Dissolve yeast in ¾ cup warm water in large mixer bowl. Beat in sugar, ½ cup margarine, the salt, eggs, egg yolk and 1¾ cups of the flour on medium speed, scraping bowl occasionally, 10 minutes. Stir in remaining flour, the almonds, fruit and lemon peel. Scrape batter from side of bowl. Cover; let rise in warm place until double, 1½ to 2 hours. (Dough is ready if indentation remains when touched with floured finger.) Stir down batter by beating about 25 strokes. Cover tightly and refrigerate at least 8 hours.

Turn dough onto well-floured surface; turn to coat with flour. Divide into halves; press each half into oval, 10x7 inches. Spread with margarine. Fold lengthwise in half; press only folded edge firmly. Place on greased cookie sheet. Beat egg white and 1 tablespoon water; brush over loaves. Let rise until double, 45 to 60 minutes. Heat oven to 375°. Bake until golden brown, 20 to 25 minutes. Drizzle with Creamy Frosting while warm.   *2 coffee cakes.*

Tutti-Frutti Coffee Cake

1 package active dry yeast	1 egg
¾ cup warm water (105 to 115°)	2¼ cups all-purpose flour
¼ cup granulated sugar	½ cup cut-up candied fruit
¼ cup shortening	¼ cup chopped nuts
1 teaspoon salt	¾ cup powdered sugar
	1 to 2 tablespoons milk

Dissolve yeast in warm water in large mixer bowl. Beat in granulated sugar, shortening, salt, egg and 1¼ cups of the flour on low speed, scraping bowl constantly, 30 seconds. Beat on medium speed, scraping bowl occasionally, 2 minutes. Stir in remaining flour, the candied fruit and nuts. Spread in greased baking pan, 9x9x2 inches. Cover; let rise in warm place until double, 1½ hours. (Dough is ready if indentation remains when touched with floured finger.)

Heat oven to 375°. Bake until golden brown, 30 to 35 minutes. Beat powdered sugar and milk until smooth and of desired consistency. Drizzle coffee cake with glaze while warm. Decorate with candied fruit and nuts if desired.

Cranberry Coffee Cake

½ Brown Sugar Sweet Dough
  (below)
1 cup cranberry-orange relish

Powdered Sugar Glaze
  (below)

Roll dough into rectangle, 12x9 inches, on lightly floured surface; transfer to greased cookie sheet. Make 3-inch diagonal cuts at 1-inch intervals on 12-inch sides of rectangle with scissors. Spread cranberry-orange relish filling down center of rectangle in 3-inch-wide strip. Crisscross strips at an angle over filling, overlapping about 1 inch (see diagram). Let rise until double, 40 to 50 minutes. Heat oven to 375°. Bake until golden brown, 20 to 25 minutes. Drizzle with Powdered Sugar Glaze while warm.

BROWN SUGAR SWEET DOUGH

2 packages active dry yeast
1 cup warm water
  (105 to 115°)
½ cup packed brown sugar
½ cup margarine or butter,
  softened

1 teaspoon salt
2 eggs
1 cup quick-cooking oats
3½ to 4 cups all-purpose flour

Dissolve yeast in warm water in large bowl. Stir in brown sugar, margarine, salt, eggs, oats and 1½ cups of the flour. Beat until smooth. Stir in enough remaining flour to make dough easy to handle.

Turn dough onto lightly floured surface; knead until smooth and elastic, about 5 minutes. Place in greased bowl; turn greased side up. Cover; let rise in warm place until double, about 1½ hours. (Dough is ready if indentation remains when touched.) Punch down dough; divide into halves.

POWDERED SUGAR GLAZE

Mix 1 cup powdered sugar and 2 to 3 teaspoons milk until smooth and of desired consistency.

Apricot-Cherry Coffee Cake: Substitute ½ cup snipped dried apricots and ½ cup chopped drained maraschino cherries for the cranberry-orange relish.

Date Coffee Cake: Substitute Date Filling for the cranberry-orange relish: Cook 1 cup cut-up dates, ⅓ cup water, 1 tablespoon sugar and 1 tablespoon grated orange peel over low heat, stirring occasionally, until thickened, about 3 minutes. Cool.

Mincemeat Coffee Cake: Substitute 1 cup prepared mincemeat for the cranberry-orange relish.

Opposite: A cranberry festival! Clockwise from top: Cranberry-Orange Muffins (page 96), Cranberry Coffee Cake (this page), Cranberry Cookies (page 23) and Cranberry-Orange Nut Bread (page 91)

Mincemeat Rolls

Roll ½ Brown Sugar Sweet Dough (page 82) into rectangle, 15x9 inches, on lightly floured surface. Spread with ⅓ cup prepared mincemeat. Roll up carefully, beginning at 15-inch side. Pinch edge of dough into roll to seal well. Stretch dough to make even. Cut into nine 1½-inch slices. Place slightly apart in greased baking pan, 9x9x2 inches. Let rise until double, about 40 minutes. Heat oven to 375°. Bake until golden brown, 25 to 30 minutes. Drizzle with Browned Butter Glaze (below) while warm. *9 rolls.*

BROWNED BUTTER GLAZE
Heat 2 tablespoons margarine or butter in 1-quart saucepan over medium heat until delicate brown; cool slightly. Stir in 1 cup powdered sugar and ½ teaspoon vanilla. Stir in 2 to 3 teaspoons milk until glaze is smooth and of desired consistency.

Cranberry Rolls: Substitute ½ cup cranberry-orange relish for the mincemeat. For the Browned Butter Glaze, substitute Orange Glaze: Mix 1 cup powdered sugar and 2 to 3 teaspoons orange juice until smooth and of desired consistency.

Cardamom-Walnut Rolls

1 package active dry yeast	1 egg
¼ cup warm water (105 to 115°)	9 cardamom seeds, crushed, or ½ teaspoon ground cardamom
1¼ cups lukewarm milk (scalded then cooled)	4¾ cups all-purpose flour
¾ cup sugar	1 egg, beaten
1 teaspoon salt	½ cup finely chopped walnuts
½ cup margarine or butter, melted	¼ cup sugar

Dissolve yeast in warm water in large bowl. Stir in milk, ¾ cup sugar, the salt, margarine, 1 egg, the cardamom seeds and 2¼ cups of the flour. Beat until smooth. Stir in remaining flour. Cover; let rise in warm place until double, about 1½ hours. (Dough is ready if indentation remains when touched.)

Turn dough onto lightly floured surface. (If necessary, work in additional flour to make dough easy to handle.) Divide dough into 15 equal parts. Roll each part into pencil-like rope, 12 inches long. Twist each into pretzel shape in greased baking pan, 13x9x2 inches. Let rise until double, about 40 minutes. Heat oven to 375°. Brush rolls with beaten egg; sprinkle with walnuts and ¼ cup sugar. Bake until golden brown, 30 to 35 minutes. *15 rolls.*

Note: For smaller rolls, divide dough into 24 equal parts. Roll each part into pencil-like rope, 8 inches long. Twist each into figure-eight shape in greased jelly roll pan, 15½x10½x1 inch. Continue as directed except—increase walnuts to ¾ cup and ¼ cup sugar to ⅓ cup. Bake 25 to 30 minutes. *2 dozen rolls.*

Overnight Cinnamon Rolls

2 packages active dry yeast
½ cup warm water
    (105 to 115°)
2 cups lukewarm milk
    (scalded then cooled)
⅓ cup sugar
⅓ cup vegetable oil or
    shortening
3 teaspoons baking powder
2 teaspoons salt

1 egg
6½ to 7½ cups all-purpose
    flour
¼ cup margarine or butter,
    softened
½ cup sugar
1 tablespoon plus 1 teaspoon
    ground cinnamon
Powdered Sugar Frosting
    (below)

Dissolve yeast in warm water in large bowl. Stir in milk, ⅓ cup sugar, the oil, baking powder, salt, egg and 3 cups of the flour. Beat until smooth. Stir in enough remaining flour to make dough easy to handle.

Turn dough onto well-floured surface; knead until smooth and elastic, 8 to 10 minutes. Place in greased bowl; turn greased side up. Cover; let rise in warm place until double, about 1½ hours. (Dough is ready if indentation remains when touched.)

Punch down dough; divide into halves. Roll 1 half into rectangle, 12x10 inches. Spread with half of the margarine. Mix ½ cup sugar and the cinnamon; sprinkle half of the sugar-cinnamon mixture over rectangle. Roll up, beginning at 12-inch side. Pinch edge of dough into roll to seal. Stretch roll to make even.

Cut roll into 12 slices. Place slightly apart in greased baking pan, 13x9x2 inches. Wrap pan tightly with heavy-duty aluminum foil. Repeat with remaining dough. Refrigerate at least 12 hours but no longer than 48 hours. (To bake immediately, do not wrap. Let rise in warm place until double, about 30 minutes. Bake as directed below.)

Heat oven to 350°. Remove foil from pans. Bake until golden, 30 to 35 minutes. Frost with Powdered Sugar Frosting while warm.
2 dozen rolls.

POWDERED SUGAR FROSTING

Mix 1 cup powdered sugar, 1 tablespoon milk and ½ teaspoon vanilla until smooth and of spreading consistency. Frosts 1 pan of rolls.

Note: If larger rolls are desired, roll into rectangles, 10x9 inches. Cut each roll into 9 slices. Place in greased baking pans, 9x9x2 inches.   *1½ dozen rolls.*

Overnight Marmalade Rolls: Omit sugar-cinnamon mixture and Powdered Sugar Frosting. Before rolling dough into rectangles, beat 2 cups powdered sugar, ½ cup orange, lime or ginger marmalade and the margarine until smooth and creamy. Spread each rectangle with ⅓ cup of the marmalade mixture. Roll dough, slice, refrigerate and bake as directed. Frost with remaining marmalade mixture while warm.

Chocolate-Cinnamon Rolls

1 package active dry yeast
¼ cup warm water
   (105 to 115°)
½ cup lukewarm milk
   (scalded then cooled)
¼ cup sugar
¼ cup shortening
1 egg
½ teaspoon salt
⅓ cup cocoa

2¼ to 2½ cups all-purpose
   flour
2 tablespoons margarine or
   butter, softened
¼ cup sugar
1½ teaspoons ground
   cinnamon
Powdered Sugar Frosting
   (page 85)

Dissolve yeast in warm water in large bowl. Stir in milk, ¼ cup sugar, the shortening, egg and salt. Mix cocoa with 1¼ cups of the flour. Add to yeast mixture. Mix with spoon until smooth. Mix in enough remaining flour to make dough easy to handle. Turn dough onto lightly floured surface; knead until smooth and elastic, about 5 minutes. Place in greased bowl; turn greased side up. (At this point, dough can be covered and refrigerated 3 to 4 days.) Cover; let rise in warm place until double, about 1½ hours. (Dough is ready if an indentation remains when touched.)

Punch down dough. Roll into rectangle, 12x9 inches. Spread with margarine. Mix ¼ cup sugar and the cinnamon; sprinkle over rectangle. Roll up, beginning at 12-inch side. Pinch edge of dough into roll to seal. Cut roll into 12 slices. Place slightly apart in greased baking pan, 9x9x2 inches. Cover; let rise until double, about 40 minutes. Heat oven to 375°. Bake 25 to 30 minutes. Spread with Powdered Sugar Frosting while warm.   *1 dozen rolls.*

Christmas Doughnuts

From the Ukraine to the Pennsylvania Dutch country, fritters and doughnuts are traditional Christmastime sweets for a number of nationalities.

1 package active dry yeast
¼ cup warm water
   (105 to 115°)
2 eggs
1 cup whipping cream
1 teaspoon vanilla
⅓ cup sugar

3½ cups all-purpose flour
3 teaspoons baking powder
1 teaspoon salt
¼ teaspoon ground
   cinnamon
¼ teaspoon ground nutmeg
Vegetable oil

Dissolve yeast in warm water in large bowl. Beat eggs, whipping cream, vanilla and sugar until light and fluffy; stir into yeast. Stir in remaining ingredients except oil until dough is soft and easy to handle.

Heat oil (2 to 3 inches) in deep-fat fryer or heavy saucepan to 375°. Roll dough ⅓ inch thick on well-floured surface. Cut with floured Christmas cookie cutters (bell, star, tree) or doughnut cutter. Slide doughnuts into hot oil with wide spatula. Fry until golden brown, about 2 minutes on each side. Remove from oil; do not prick doughnuts. Drain on paper towels. Serve plain, sugared or frosted.
2 dozen doughnuts.

Snowman Buns

1 package active dry yeast	2 teaspoons ground nutmeg, if desired
¾ cup warm water (105 to 115°)	1 teaspoon salt
⅓ cup sugar	3½ cups all-purpose flour
¼ cup shortening	24 currants
2 eggs	1 egg, slightly beaten

Dissolve yeast in warm water in large mixer bowl. Add sugar, shortening, 2 eggs, the nutmeg, salt and 2 cups of the flour. Beat on low speed, scraping bowl constantly, 30 seconds. Beat on medium speed, scraping bowl occasionally, 2 minutes. Stir in remaining flour until smooth. Cover; let rise in warm place until double, about 45 minutes. (Dough is ready if indentation remains when touched with floured finger.)

Stir down dough by beating 25 strokes. Turn onto well-floured surface; cut into 12 equal parts (each part will make 1 snowman). Shape ½ of each part into 4-inch oval for the body. Shape ½ of the remaining dough into ball for the head. Press in tiny piece of dough for nose. Shape remaining dough into 4-inch roll and cut into halves for arms.

Arrange snowmen about 3 inches apart on greased cookie sheet. Let rise until double, about 45 minutes. Press in 2 currants for eyes and 3 for buttons. Heat oven to 350°. Brush snowmen with beaten egg. Bake until golden brown, about 15 minutes. Decorate with Creamy Decorators' Frosting (page 7) if desired.   *1 dozen buns.*

Snowman Buns are an adaptation of a New Year's bread that originated in St. Albans, England. Tradition has it that the little breads were called ''Pope Ladies'' for the mythical Popess Joan of 858 A.D.

Refrigerator Roll Dough

1 package active dry yeast	⅔ cup sugar
1½ cups warm water	⅔ cup shortening
(105 to 115°)	2 eggs
1 cup unseasoned lukewarm	1½ teaspoons salt
mashed potatoes	6 to 7 cups all-purpose flour

Dissolve yeast in warm water in large bowl. Stir in potatoes, sugar, shortening, eggs, salt and 3 cups of the flour. Beat until smooth. Stir in enough remaining flour to make dough easy to handle.

Turn dough onto lightly floured surface; knead until smooth and elastic, about 5 minutes. Place in greased bowl; turn greased side up. Cover bowl tightly; refrigerate at least 8 hours but no longer than 5 days.

Punch down dough; divide into 4 equal parts. Use ¼ of the dough for any Dinner Roll recipe (below).

Whole Wheat Refrigerator Roll Dough: Substitute 3 to 4 cups whole wheat flour for the second addition of all-purpose flour.

DINNER ROLLS

Brown-and-Serve Rolls: Shape Refrigerator Roll Dough (above) as directed in any roll recipe below. Let rise 1 hour. Heat oven to 275°. Bake 20 minutes (do not allow to brown). Remove from pans; cool to room temperature. Wrap in aluminum foil. Store in refrigerator no longer than 8 days or freeze no longer than 2 months. At serving time, heat oven to 400°. Bake until brown, 8 to 12 minutes.

Casseroles: Shape ¼ of Refrigerator Roll Dough (above) into 1-inch balls. Place in lightly greased round layer pan, 9x1½ inches. Brush with margarine or butter, softened. Let rise 1 hour. Heat oven to 400°. Bake until golden brown, about 15 minutes.   *3 dozen rolls.*

Cloverleaf Rolls: Shape ¼ of Refrigerator Roll Dough (above) into 1-inch balls. Place 3 balls in each greased medium muffin cup, 2½x1¼ inches. Brush with margarine or butter, softened. Let rise 1 hour. Heat oven to 400°. Bake until golden brown, 15 to 20 minutes.   *1 dozen rolls.*

Crescent Rolls: Roll ¼ of Refrigerator Roll Dough (above) into 12-inch circle on floured surface. Spread with margarine, softened. Cut into 16 wedges. Roll up tightly, beginning at rounded edges, stretching dough as it is rolled. Place rolls with points underneath on greased cookie sheet; curve slightly. Brush with margarine, softened. Let rise 1 hour. Heat oven to 400°. Bake 15 minutes. *16 rolls.*

Four-Leaf Clovers: Shape ¼ of Refrigerator Roll Dough (above) into 2-inch balls. Place each ball in greased medium muffin cup, 2½x1¼ inches. With scissors, snip each ball completely into halves, then into quarters. Brush with margarine or butter, softened. Let rise 1 hour. Heat oven to 400°. Bake until golden brown, 15 to 20 minutes.   *8 to 10 rolls.*

Squash Rolls

1 cup milk	¼ cup warm water
½ cup sugar	(105 to 115°)
2 tablespoons margarine or	1 cup mashed cooked winter
butter	squash*
1 teaspoon salt	4½ to 5 cups all-purpose flour
1 package active dry yeast	

Heat milk, sugar, margarine and salt until margarine is melted. Cool to lukewarm. Dissolve yeast in warm water in large bowl. Stir in milk mixture, squash and 2 cups of the flour. Beat until smooth. Stir in enough remaining flour to make dough easy to handle.

Turn dough onto lightly floured surface; knead until smooth and elastic, about 5 minutes. Place in greased bowl; turn greased side up. Cover; let rise in warm place until double, about 1½ hours. (Dough is ready if indentation remains when touched.)

Punch down dough. Shape into 1-inch balls. Place 3 balls in each of 24 greased medium muffin cups, 2½x1¼ inches. Let rise until double, 30 to 45 minutes. Heat oven to 400°. Bake until golden brown, 15 to 20 minutes.   *2 dozen rolls.*

*1 cup frozen squash, thawed and brought to room temperature, can be substituted for the fresh squash.

Pumpkin Crescents

1 package active dry yeast	1 egg
1 cup warm water	1½ teaspoons salt
(105 to 115°)	5 to 6 cups all-purpose flour
1 cup canned pumpkin	Margarine or butter,
½ cup shortening	softened
⅓ cup sugar	

Dissolve yeast in warm water in large bowl. Stir in pumpkin, shortening, sugar, egg, salt and 3 cups of the flour. Beat until smooth. Stir in enough remaining flour to make dough easy to handle.

Turn dough onto lightly floured surface; knead until smooth and elastic, about 5 minutes. Place in greased bowl; turn greased side up. Cover; let rise in warm place until double, about 1 hour. (Dough is ready if indentation remains when touched.)

Punch down dough; divide into 3 equal parts. Roll each part into 12-inch circle on floured surface. Spread with margarine; cut into 12 wedges. Roll up tightly, beginning at rounded edges. Place rolls with points underneath on greased cookie sheet; curve slightly. Let rise until double, 30 to 45 minutes. Heat oven to 400°. Bake until golden brown, 15 to 20 minutes.   *3 dozen rolls.*

Sweet Potato Crescents: Substitute 1 cup lukewarm mashed sweet potatoes for the canned pumpkin.

Pumpkin Crescents

Cranberry-Orange Nut Bread

2 cups all-purpose flour	1 tablespoon grated orange
¾ cup sugar	peel
1½ teaspoons baking powder	¾ cup orange juice
¾ teaspoon salt	1 egg
½ teaspoon baking soda	1 cup cranberries, chopped
¼ cup margarine or butter, softened	½ cup chopped nuts

Heat oven to 350°. Grease bottom only of loaf pan, 9x5x3 inches. Mix flour, sugar, baking powder, salt and baking soda. Stir in margarine until mixture is crumbly. Stir in orange peel, orange juice and egg just until all flour is moistened. Stir in cranberries and nuts. Pour into pan. Bake until wooden pick inserted in center comes out clean, 55 to 65 minutes. Loosen sides of loaf from pan; remove from pan. Cool completely before slicing.

Poppy Seed Bread

2½ cups all-purpose flour	1¼ cups milk
1 cup sugar	⅓ cup vegetable oil
¼ cup poppy seed	1 egg
3½ teaspoons baking powder	1 teaspoon vanilla
1 teaspoon salt	

Heat oven to 350°. Grease bottom only of loaf pan, 9x5x3 inches, or 2 loaf pans, 8½x4½x2½ inches. Mix all ingredients; beat 30 seconds. Pour into pan(s). Bake until wooden pick inserted in center comes out clean, 9-inch loaf 55 to 65 minutes, 8½-inch loaves 55 to 60 minutes. Cool slightly. Loosen sides of loaf from pan; remove from pan. Cool completely before slicing. To store, wrap and refrigerate no longer than 1 week.   *1 large or 2 small loaves*.

Pumpkin-Date Bread

2½ cups sugar	1½ teaspoons salt
⅔ cup vegetable oil	1 teaspoon ground
4 eggs	cinnamon
1 can (16 ounces) pumpkin	1 teaspoon ground cloves
⅔ cup water	½ teaspoon baking powder
3⅓ cups all-purpose flour	½ cup coarsely chopped nuts
2 teaspoons baking soda	½ cup cut-up dates

Heat oven to 350°. Grease bottoms only of 2 loaf pans, 9x5x3 inches, or 3 loaf pans, 8½x4½x2½ inches. Mix sugar, oil, eggs, pumpkin and water in large bowl. Stir in remaining ingredients. Pour into pans. Bake until wooden pick inserted in center comes out clean, about 1 hour 10 minutes; cool slightly. Loosen sides of loaves from pans; remove from pans. Cool completely before slicing. To store, wrap and refrigerate no longer than 10 days.   *2 large or 3 small loaves*.

Opposite: The delicious bounty of a winter baking day. Left to right: Poppy Seed Bread (this page), Apple-Raisin Bread (page 93) and Cherry Nut Bread (page 92)

Holiday Nut Bread

2½ cups all-purpose flour	2 eggs
1¼ cups buttermilk*	3 teaspoons baking powder
½ cup granulated sugar	1 teaspoon salt
½ cup packed brown sugar	½ teaspoon baking soda
¼ cup shortening	1 cup chopped nuts

Heat oven to 350°. Grease bottom only of loaf pan, 9x5x3 inches. Beat all ingredients in large mixer bowl on low speed 15 seconds. Beat on medium speed, scraping bowl constantly, 30 seconds. Pour into pan. Bake until wooden pick inserted in center comes out clean, 60 to 65 minutes. Immediately remove from pan; cool completely on wire rack. Garnish top of nut bread with maraschino cherries and sliced green candied pineapple if desired. For best results, wrap and refrigerate at least 8 hours before slicing.

*1¼ cups milk and 1 tablespoon vinegar can be substituted for the buttermilk. Mix and let stand 5 minutes.

Banana Nut Bread: Substitute 1¼ cups mashed bananas and ⅓ cup whole milk for the buttermilk. Bake 70 to 75 minutes.

Cherry Nut Bread: Reduce buttermilk to 1 cup and add ¼ cup maraschino cherry juice. After beating, stir in ½ cup chopped drained maraschino cherries. Bake 70 to 75 minutes.

Date Nut Bread: Substitute date mixture for the buttermilk. For date mixture, add 1½ cups boiling water to 1½ cups cut-up dates. Stir and let cool. Bake 65 to 70 minutes.

Gumdrop Bread

2½ cups all-purpose flour	1 teaspoon salt
1¼ cups buttermilk	1 teaspoon vanilla
½ cup granulated sugar	½ teaspoon baking soda
½ cup packed brown sugar	1 cup small gumdrops,
¼ cup shortening	cut into halves
2 eggs	½ cup chopped nuts,
3 teaspoons baking powder	if desired

Heat oven to 350°. Grease bottom only of loaf pan, 9x5x3 inches. Beat all ingredients except gumdrops and nuts in large mixer bowl on low speed 15 seconds. Beat on medium speed, scraping bowl constantly, 30 seconds. Stir in gumdrops and nuts; pour into pan. Bake until wooden pick inserted in center comes out clean, 60 to 65 minutes. Loosen sides of loaf from pan; remove from pan. Cool completely on wire rack. For best results, store bread at least 24 hours before slicing. To store, wrap and refrigerate no longer than 1 week.

Little Gumdrop Loaves: Substitute 6 well-greased 10½-ounce soup cans (1¼-cup capacity) for the loaf pan. Divide batter among soup cans. Bake about 40 minutes. *6 loaves.*

Little Gumdrop Loaves

Carrot-Raisin Bread

3 eggs	2 teaspoons baking soda
1½ cups vegetable oil	1 teaspoon baking powder
2 cups shredded carrots	1 teaspoon salt
1½ cups sugar	1 teaspoon ground cinnamon
2 tablespoons grated orange peel	1 teaspoon ground cloves
	⅔ cup chopped nuts
1 teaspoon vanilla	⅔ cup raisins
3⅓ cups all-purpose flour	

Heat oven to 350°. Grease bottoms only of 2 loaf pans, 9x5x3 inches. Beat eggs, oil, carrots, sugar, orange peel and vanilla on low speed, scraping bowl occasionally, 1 minute. Add flour, baking soda, baking powder, salt, cinnamon and cloves. Beat on low speed, scraping bowl occasionally, until moistened, about 15 seconds. Beat on medium speed 45 seconds. Stir in nuts and raisins. Spread in pans. Bake until wooden pick inserted in center comes out clean, 55 to 60 minutes. Cool 10 minutes; remove from pans. Cool completely before slicing. To store, wrap and refrigerate.   *2 loaves.*

Apple-Raisin Bread: Substitute 2 cups chopped unpared apples for the carrots. Omit orange peel.

Mincemeat Coffee Ring

2 cups all-purpose flour	⅔ cup milk
2 tablespoons sugar	⅓ cup vegetable oil
3 teaspoons baking powder	1 cup prepared mincemeat
1 teaspoon salt	Lemon Glaze (below)

Heat oven to 425°. Mix flour, sugar, baking powder and salt. Stir in milk and oil until dough leaves side of bowl and rounds up into a ball. Knead lightly 10 times. Roll into rectangle, 13x9 inches, on lightly floured surface. Spread with mincemeat. Roll up tightly, beginning at 13-inch side. Pinch edge of dough into roll to seal.

With sealed edge down, shape into ring on lightly greased cookie sheet. Pinch ends together. With scissors, make cuts ⅔ of the way through ring at 1-inch intervals. Turn each section on its side. Bake until golden brown, 20 to 25 minutes. Spread with Lemon Glaze while warm.   *8 to 10 servings.*

LEMON GLAZE
Beat ½ cup powdered sugar and 1 to 2 teaspoons lemon juice until smooth and of desired consistency.

Jam Tea Ring: Substitute ⅓ cup jam for the mincemeat.

Sour Cream Coffee Cake

1½ cups sugar
¾ cup margarine or butter, softened
3 eggs
1½ teaspoons vanilla
3 cups all-purpose or whole wheat flour
1½ teaspoons baking powder
1½ teaspoons baking soda
¾ teaspoon salt
1½ cups dairy sour cream
Filling (below)
Light Brown Glaze (below)

Heat oven to 350°. Grease tube pan, 10x4 inches, 12-cup bundt cake pan or 2 loaf pans, 9x5x3 inches. Beat sugar, margarine, eggs and vanilla in large mixer bowl on medium speed, scraping bowl occasionally, 2 minutes. Beat in flour, baking powder, baking soda and salt alternately with sour cream on low speed. Prepare Filling.

For tube or bundt cake, spread ⅓ of the batter (about 2 cups) in pan and sprinkle with ⅓ of the Filling (about 6 tablespoons); repeat 2 times. For loaves, spread ¼ of the batter (about 1½ cups) in each pan and sprinkle each with ¼ of the Filling (about 5 tablespoons); repeat.

Bake until wooden pick inserted near center comes out clean, about 1 hour. Cool slightly; remove from pan(s). Cool 10 minutes; drizzle with Light Brown Glaze.   *14 to 16 servings.*

FILLING
Mix ½ cup packed brown sugar, ½ cup finely chopped nuts and 1½ teaspoons ground cinnamon.

LIGHT BROWN GLAZE
¼ cup margarine or butter
2 cups powdered sugar
1 teaspoon vanilla
1 to 2 tablespoons milk

Heat margarine in 1½-quart saucepan over medium heat until delicate brown. Stir in powdered sugar and vanilla. Stir in milk, 1 tablespoon at a time, until glaze is smooth and of desired consistency.

Cranberry-Orange Coffee Cake

2 cups buttermilk baking mix
⅔ cup orange juice
½ cup chopped cranberries
3 tablespoons sugar
2 tablespoons vegetable oil
1 egg
Orange Frosting (below)

Heat oven to 400°. Mix all ingredients except Orange Frosting; beat 30 seconds. Pour into greased round layer pan, 9x1½ inches. Bake until golden brown, 25 to 30 minutes. Spread with frosting while warm.   *8 to 12 servings.*

ORANGE FROSTING
Mix ½ cup powdered sugar and 2 to 3 teaspoons orange juice until smooth and of desired consistency.

Holiday Streusel Coffee Cake

Streusel (below)
2 cups all-purpose flour
1 cup sugar
3 teaspoons baking powder
1 teaspoon salt
⅓ cup margarine or butter,
    softened
1 cup milk
1 egg
⅔ cup cut-up candied fruit

Heat oven to 350°. Prepare Streusel. Beat remaining ingredients except candied fruit in large mixer bowl on low speed 30 seconds. Beat on medium speed, scraping bowl occasionally, 2 minutes. Stir in candied fruit. Spread batter in greased baking pan, 13x9x2 inches; sprinkle with Streusel. Bake until wooden pick inserted in center comes out clean, 35 to 40 minutes.   *12 servings.*

STREUSEL
½ cup chopped nuts
⅓ cup packed brown sugar
¼ cup all-purpose flour
½ teaspoon ground cinnamon
3 tablespoons firm margarine
    or butter

Mix all ingredients until crumbly.

Note: For 2 small coffee cakes, divide batter between 2 greased 8-inch round layer or 8-inch square pans. Sprinkle each with half of the streusel mixture. Bake until wooden pick inserted in center comes out clean, 25 to 30 minutes.

Cinnamon 'n Sugar Muffins

2 eggs
½ cup milk
¼ cup applesauce
¼ cup margarine or butter,
    melted
2 cups all-purpose flour
½ cup raisins
¼ cup sugar
1 teaspoon baking powder
½ teaspoon salt
½ teaspoon ground cinnamon
¼ cup sugar
¾ teaspoon ground cinnamon
¼ cup margarine or butter,
    melted

Heat oven to 400°. Grease bottoms only of 12 medium muffin cups, 2½x1¼ inches. Beat eggs; stir in milk, applesauce and ¼ cup margarine. Stir in flour, raisins, ¼ cup sugar, the baking powder, salt and ½ teaspoon cinnamon all at once just until flour is moistened (batter will be lumpy).

Fill muffin cups about ⅔ full. Bake until golden brown, 20 to 25 minutes. Mix ¼ cup sugar and ¾ teaspoon cinnamon. Immediately dip tops of warm muffins into melted margarine, then into sugar-cinnamon mixture.   *1 dozen muffins.*

Cinnamon-Apple Muffins: Fill muffin cups ⅓ full. Spoon 1 teaspoon applesauce onto batter in each cup; top with enough batter to fill cups about ⅔ full.

Cinnamon 'n Sugar Muffins

Cranberry-Orange Muffins

1 egg	2 cups all-purpose flour
1 cup milk	¼ cup sugar
1 cup fresh or frozen cranberries, cut into halves	1 tablespoon grated orange peel
¼ cup vegetable oil	3 teaspoons baking powder
	1 teaspoon salt

Heat oven to 400°. Grease bottoms only of 12 medium muffin cups, 2½x1¼ inches. Beat egg; stir in milk, cranberries and oil. Stir in remaining ingredients all at once just until flour is moistened (batter will be lumpy). Fill muffin cups ⅔ full. Bake until golden brown, 20 to 25 minutes. Immediately remove from pan.   *1 dozen muffins.*

Pumpkin Muffins

1 egg	½ cup sugar
½ cup milk	2 teaspoons baking powder
½ cup canned pumpkin	½ teaspoon salt
½ cup raisins	½ teaspoon ground cinnamon
¼ cup margarine or butter, melted	½ teaspoon ground nutmeg
1½ cups all-purpose flour	

Heat oven to 400°. Grease bottoms only of 12 medium muffin cups, 2½x1¼ inches. Beat egg; stir in milk, pumpkin, raisins and margarine. Stir in remaining ingredients all at once just until flour is moistened (batter will be lumpy). Fill muffin cups ⅔ full. Sprinkle ¼ teaspoon sugar over batter in each cup if desired. Bake until golden brown, about 20 minutes.   *1 dozen muffins.*

Yam Muffins: Substitute ½ cup mashed cooked yams or sweet potatoes for the pumpkin. Omit raisins and, if desired, add ½ cup chopped pecans or walnuts.

Opposite: Roast Turkey (page 98)

Holiday Fare for Family and Friends

Christmas Day Dinners

Whether you stay with tradition or search for something out of the ordinary, you'll find a fitting menu for your plans. Choose a turkey or roast when you're celebrating with a number of guests, or try salmon steaks or a crown of spareribs for a smaller splurge. Remember these menus, too, for gala dinner parties throughout the holiday season.

MENU

ZESTY BEEF BROTH

ROAST TURKEY

GIBLET GRAVY

OLD-FASHIONED
BREAD STUFFING

MASHED POTATOES

BROCCOLI SPEARS

DELUXE CREAMED ONIONS

FRESH CRANBERRY SALAD

SWEET POTATO CRESCENTS
(PAGE 89)

APPLE-MINCE PIE (PAGE 66)

8 SERVINGS

Zesty Beef Broth

2 cans (10½ ounces each) condensed beef broth (about 2½ cups)
1 cup tomato juice, if desired
1 cup water
1½ teaspoons prepared horseradish
½ teaspoon dried dill weed

Heat all ingredients to simmering. Serve hot or cold. Allow about ½ cup for each serving.

Roast Turkey

When buying turkeys under 12 pounds, allow about ¾ pound per serving. For heavier turkeys (12 pounds and over) allow about ½ pound per serving.

Rub cavity of turkey lightly with salt if desired. Do not salt cavity if turkey is to be stuffed. Stuff turkey just before roasting—not ahead of time. (See Old-Fashioned Bread Stuffing, page 100.) Fill wishbone area with stuffing first. Fasten neck skin to back with skewer. Fold wings across back with tips touching. Fill body cavity lightly. (Do not pack—stuffing will expand while cooking.) Tuck drumsticks under band of skin at tail or tie together with heavy string, then tie to tail.

Place turkey breast side up on rack in shallow roasting pan. Brush with shortening, oil, margarine or butter. Insert meat thermometer so tip is in thickest part of inside thigh muscle or thickest part of breast meat and does not touch bone. Do not add water.

Roast uncovered in 325° oven. Follow Timetable (below) for approximate total cooking time. Place a tent of aluminum foil loosely over turkey when it begins to turn golden. When ⅔ done, cut band of skin or string holding legs.

TIMETABLE FOR ROASTING TURKEY

Ready-to-Cook Weight	Approximate Total Cooking Time	Internal Temperature (°F)
6 to 8 pounds	3 to 3½ hours	185°
8 to 12 pounds	3½ to 4½ hours	185°
12 to 16 pounds	4½ to 5½ hours	185°
16 to 20 pounds	5½ to 6½ hours	185°
20 to 24 pounds	6½ to 7 hours	185°

This timetable is based on chilled or completely thawed stuffed turkeys at a temperature of about 40°. Time will be slightly less for unstuffed turkeys. Differences in the shape and tenderness of individual turkeys can also necessitate increasing or decreasing the cooking time slightly. For best results, use a meat thermometer. For prestuffed turkeys, follow package directions very carefully; do not use Timetable.

There is no substitute for a meat thermometer for determining the doneness of a turkey. Placed in the thigh muscle, it should register 185° when turkey is done. If turkey is stuffed, the thermometer point can be inserted in the center of stuffing and will register 165° when done. If a thermometer is not used, test for doneness about 30 minutes before Timetable so indicates. Move drumstick up and down—if done, the joint should give readily or break. Or press drumstick meat between fingers; meat should be very soft.

When turkey is done, remove from oven and allow to stand about 20 minutes for easiest carving. As soon as possible after serving, remove every bit of stuffing from turkey. Cool stuffing, turkey meat and any gravy promptly; refrigerate separately. Use gravy or stuffing within 1 or 2 days; heat them thoroughly before serving. Serve cooked turkey meat within 2 or 3 days after roasting. If frozen, it can be kept up to 3 weeks.

Roast Turkey Breast

Prepare turkey breast according to basic instructions for whole turkey except—skewer skin to meat along cut edges to prevent shrinking from meat during roasting. Place skin side up on rack in shallow roasting pan. Place meat thermometer in thickest part. Be sure it does not touch bone. Brush with vegetable oil. Roast uncovered in 325° oven until thermometer registers 180 to 185°, 1½ to 2¼ hours for 5- to 8-pound breast, 2¼ to 3½ hours for 8- to 10-pound breast.

Giblet Gravy

Cover turkey gizzard, heart and neck with water. Sprinkle with ½ teaspoon salt and ¼ teaspoon pepper. Heat to boiling; reduce heat. Simmer uncovered until gizzard is fork-tender, 1 to 1½ hours. Add the liver during the last 5 to 10 minutes of cooking. Drain; reserve broth for gravy. Cut up giblets. Refrigerate broth and giblets until ready to use.

Pour drippings from roasting pan into bowl. Return ½ cup drippings to pan. Stir in ½ cup all-purpose flour. Cook over low heat, stirring constantly, until mixture is smooth and bubbly; remove from heat. Add enough water to reserved broth to measure 4 cups. Stir into flour mixture. Heat to boiling, stirring constantly. Boil and stir 1 minute. Stir in giblets; sprinkle with salt and pepper. Heat until giblets are hot.   *4 cups gravy.*

Old-Fashioned Bread Stuffing

How much stuffing should you make? Allow ¾ cup for each pound of ready-to-cook turkey. This recipe makes enough for a 12-pounder.

1½ cups chopped celery (with leaves)	1½ teaspoons dried sage leaves
¾ cup finely chopped onion	1 teaspoon dried thyme leaves
1 cup margarine or butter	½ teaspoon pepper
9 cups soft bread cubes	
1½ teaspoons salt	

Cook and stir celery and onion in margarine in 10-inch skillet until onion is tender. Stir in about ⅓ of the bread cubes. Pour into deep bowl. Add remaining ingredients; toss. Stuff turkey just before roasting.   *9 cups stuffing.*

Note: To cook stuffing separately, place in greased 3-quart casserole or baking dish, 13x9x2 inches. Cover and cook in 325° oven 45 minutes. Uncover during last 15 minutes.

Chestnut Stuffing: Decrease bread cubes to 7 cups and add 1 pound chestnuts, cooked and chopped, with the remaining ingredients. To prepare chestnuts, cut an "X" on rounded side of each chestnut. Heat chestnuts and enough water to cover to boiling. Boil uncovered 10 minutes; drain. Remove shells and skins. Heat chestnuts and enough water to cover to boiling. Boil uncovered 10 minutes; drain and chop.

Corn Bread Stuffing: Substitute corn bread cubes for the soft bread cubes.

Oyster Stuffing: Decrease bread cubes to 8 cups and add 2 cans (8 ounces each) oysters, drained and chopped, with the remaining ingredients.

Sausage Stuffing: Decrease bread cubes to 8 cups and omit salt. Add 1 pound bulk pork sausage, crumbled and browned, with the remaining ingredients. Substitute sausage drippings for part of the margarine.

Mashed Potatoes

3 pounds potatoes (about 9 medium)
½ to ¾ cup milk
⅓ cup margarine or butter, softened
¾ teaspoon salt
Dash of pepper

If you have a microwave, put it to use for just-before-serving reheating (see tip).

Heat 1 inch salted water (½ teaspoon salt to 1 cup water) to boiling. Add potatoes. Cover and heat to boiling. Cook until tender, whole 30 to 35 minutes, pieces 20 to 25 minutes; drain. Shake pan gently over low heat to dry potatoes. Mash potatoes until no lumps remain. Beat in milk in small amounts. Add margarine, salt and pepper; beat vigorously until potatoes are light and fluffy.

☐ **Microwave Tip:** Prepare mashed potatoes ahead of time. Place in microwaveproof serving dish, cover and refrigerate. To reheat, cover and microwave on high (100%) until hot, 8 to 10 minutes, stirring once.

Deluxe Creamed Onions

2 pounds small white onions*
2 tablespoons margarine or butter
2 tablespoons flour
½ teaspoon salt
⅛ teaspoon pepper
1½ cups half-and-half
1½ cups shredded carrots

Heat several inches salted water (½ teaspoon salt to 1 cup water) to boiling. Add onions. Cover and heat to boiling. Cook until tender, small 15 to 20 minutes, large 30 to 35 minutes; drain.

Heat margarine over low heat until melted. Blend in flour, salt and pepper. Cook over low heat, stirring constantly, until mixture is smooth and bubbly; remove from heat. Stir in half-and-half. Heat to boiling, stirring constantly. Boil and stir 1 minute. Stir in carrots and cook 5 minutes longer. Pour sauce over hot onions.

*2 cans (16 ounces each) whole onions, heated and drained, can be substituted for the cooked fresh onions.

Fresh Cranberry Salad

2 cups water
¾ cup sugar
3 cups cranberries (12 ounces)
1 package (6 ounces) orange-flavored gelatin
1 can (8¼ ounces) crushed pineapple
½ cup chopped celery or walnuts
Salad greens

Heat water and sugar to boiling in 2-quart saucepan; boil 1 minute. Add cranberries. Heat to boiling; boil 5 minutes. Stir in gelatin until dissolved. Stir in pineapple (with syrup) and celery. Pour into 6-cup mold or 8 individual molds. Refrigerate until firm, at least 6 hours. Unmold on salad greens. Garnish with dairy sour cream and pineapple chunks if desired.

Fresh Cranberry Salad

Roast Goose with Browned Potatoes

1 goose (9 to 11 pounds)
4 to 6 large potatoes, pared and cut into halves
Salt and pepper
Paprika

Trim excess fat from goose. Rub cavity of goose lightly with salt. Fasten neck skin of goose to back with skewer. Fold wings across back with tips touching. Tie drumsticks to tail. Prick skin all over with fork. Place goose breast side up on rack in shallow roasting pan. Roast uncovered in 350° oven until done, 3 to 3½ hours, removing excess fat from pan occasionally.

One hour and 15 minutes before goose is done, place potatoes in roasting pan around goose. Brush potatoes with goose fat; sprinkle with salt, pepper and paprika. If necessary, place a tent of aluminum foil loosely over goose to prevent excessive browning. Goose is done when drumstick meat feels very soft. Place goose and potatoes on heated platter. Cover and let stand 15 minutes for easier carving. Garnish with kumquats and parsley if desired.

Note: To carve, remove the wings and legs. Cut away each breast half in one piece. Slice the breast meat, thighs and drumsticks into smaller portions.

MENU

ROAST GOOSE
WITH BROWNED POTATOES

APPLE-RAISIN DRESSING

BRAISED RED CABBAGE

HOLIDAY SALAD

CLOVERLEAF ROLLS (PAGE 88)

CHRISTMAS STEAMED
PUDDING (PAGE 57)

6 TO 8 SERVINGS

Apple-Raisin Dressing

1½ cups chopped celery (with leaves)
1 medium onion, chopped
1 cup margarine or butter
8 cups soft bread cubes
3 tart apples, chopped
½ cup raisins
1½ teaspoons salt
1½ teaspoons dried sage leaves
¼ teaspoon pepper

Cook and stir celery and onion in margarine in 10-inch skillet until onion is tender. Stir in about ⅓ of the bread cubes. Pour into deep bowl. Add remaining ingredients; toss. Place in greased baking pan, 13x9x2 inches, or 3-quart casserole. Cover and cook in 350° oven 15 minutes. Uncover and cook until hot and slightly crisp, about 15 minutes longer.   *6 cups dressing*.

Braised Red Cabbage

1 medium head red cabbage, coarsely shredded (about 10 cups)
⅓ cup water
⅓ cup vinegar
3 tablespoons sugar
1½ teaspoons salt
¼ teaspoon pepper

Heat all ingredients to boiling in Dutch oven, stirring occasionally; reduce heat. Cover and simmer until cabbage is tender, about 25 minutes.

Holiday Salad

2 cups boiling water
1 package (6 ounces)
    lime-flavored gelatin
1 can (20 ounces) crushed
    pineapple, drained
    (reserve syrup)
1 package (8 ounces) cream
    cheese, softened

¾ cup whipping cream
½ cup finely chopped celery
2 tablespoons mayonnaise or
    salad dressing
   Salad greens

Pour boiling water on gelatin in 1½-quart bowl; stir until gelatin is dissolved. Add enough water to reserved pineapple syrup to measure 1 cup; stir into gelatin. Pour ½ cup gelatin into 7-cup mold or baking pan, 9x9x2 inches. Refrigerate until firm.

Gradually beat remaining gelatin into cream cheese until smooth. Refrigerate until slightly thickened, 1 to 1½ hours. Beat until smooth. Beat whipping cream in chilled bowl until stiff. Fold pineapple, whipped cream, celery and mayonnaise into gelatin mixture. Pour over gelatin in mold. Refrigerate until firm, at least 2 hours. Unmold on salad greens.

MENU

HOT SHERRIED MADRILENE

ROAST BEEF
WITH YORKSHIRE PUDDING

BRUSSELS SPROUTS
WITH CELERY

ORANGE-KIWI-GRAPE SALAD

PARKERHOUSE ROLLS

RASPBERRY TRIFLE (PAGE 59)

8 SERVINGS

Hot Sherried Madrilene

Heat 2 cans (13 ounces each) clear madrilene and 1 can (13 ounces) red madrilene to boiling. Remove from heat; stir in ⅓ cup sherry or other dry white wine. Garnish with thin lemon slices if desired. Allow about ⅔ cup for each serving.

☐ **Microwave Directions:** Pour madrilene into 1½-quart microwaveproof casserole. Cover tightly and microwave on high (100%) to boiling, 7 to 9 minutes. Stir in wine.

Roast Beef with Yorkshire Pudding

Place 4- to 6-pound boneless rib roast fat side up on rack in shallow roasting pan. Sprinkle with salt and pepper. Insert meat thermometer so tip is in center of thickest part of beef and does not rest in fat. Do not add water.

Roast uncovered in 325° oven to desired degree of doneness: 130 to 135° for rare, about 1¾ hours; 150 to 155° for medium, about 2¼ hours. (See note.) About 5 minutes before beef reaches desired temperature, prepare Yorkshire Pudding Batter (page 105). Remove beef from oven; increase oven temperature to 425°. Heat baking pan, 9x9x2 inches, in oven. Transfer beef to platter; cover with aluminum foil. Pour off drippings and add enough vegetable oil, if necessary, to measure ¼ cup. Place hot drippings in heated pan; pour in pudding batter. Bake until puffed and golden brown, about 25 minutes. Cut into squares; serve with sliced roast beef.

YORKSHIRE PUDDING BATTER

1 cup all-purpose flour	2 eggs
1 cup milk	½ teaspoon salt

Mix all ingredients with hand beater just until smooth.

Note: Roasts are easier to carve if allowed to set 20 minutes after removing from oven. Meat continues to cook as it stands; to allow for this, the internal temperatures given in the recipe are 5 to 10 degrees below the meat thermometer markings for rare and medium beef.

Brussels Sprouts with Celery

Cook 2 packages (10 ounces each) frozen Brussels sprouts as directed on package except—stir in 1½ cups thinly sliced celery during last 4 to 5 minutes of cooking. Cover and cook until Brussels sprouts are tender and celery is crisp-tender; drain. Stir in 3 tablespoons margarine or butter and ⅛ teaspoon pepper.

☐ **Microwave Directions:** Place margarine, pepper, ½ teaspoon salt and the Brussels sprouts in 2-quart microwaveproof casserole. Cover tightly and microwave on high (100%) 7 minutes; stir in celery. Cover and microwave until Brussels sprouts are tender and celery is crisp-tender, 4 to 7 minutes longer.

Orange-Kiwi-Grape Salad

4 oranges, pared and sliced	Honey-Spice Dressing
2 kiwi, pared and sliced	(below)
Salad greens	
1 cup fresh seedless green	
grapes, halved	

Arrange orange and kiwi slices on salad greens; top with grapes. Serve with Honey-Spice Dressing.

HONEY-SPICE DRESSING

Mix ¼ cup lemon juice, ¼ cup honey and ½ teaspoon ground cinnamon.

Citrus-Avocado Salad: Substitute 1 grapefruit, pared and sectioned, and 1 avocado, sliced, for the kiwi and grapes.

Orange-Apple-Grape Salad: Substitute 2 medium apples, thinly sliced, for the kiwi.

Hot Sherried Madrilene

Tomato Bouillon

Heat 3 cups tomato juice, 1 can (10½ ounces) condensed beef broth, ½ teaspoon prepared horseradish and ¼ teaspoon celery salt over low heat 15 minutes. Allow about ½ cup for each serving.

Roast Leg of Lamb

Select a 5- to 7-pound leg of lamb. Do not remove fell (paperlike covering). Make 4 or 5 small slits in lamb with tip of knife; insert slivers of garlic into slits. Sprinkle lamb with salt and pepper. Place lamb fat side up on rack in shallow roasting pan. Insert meat thermometer so tip is in center of thickest part of lamb and does not touch bone or rest in fat. Do not add water. Roast uncovered in 325° oven until thermometer registers 170°, about 2½ hours for 5-pound roast, about 3½ hours for 7-pound roast. Lamb can also be roasted to 140° (rare) or 160° (medium).

Note: Roasts are easier to carve if allowed to set 15 to 20 minutes after removing from oven. Since meat continues to cook after removal from oven, if roast is to set, it should be removed from oven when thermometer registers 5° lower than desired doneness.

Hot Minted Fruit

⅔ cup mint-flavored jelly
2 tablespoons margarine or
    butter
2 tablespoons lemon juice
1 can (20 ounces) pineapple
    chunks, drained

2 cans (16 ounces each) pear
    halves, drained and cut
    into fourths

Cook and stir jelly, margarine and lemon juice in 2-quart saucepan until jelly is melted. Stir in pineapple and pears; heat over low heat until fruit is hot, about 10 minutes.

☐ **Microwave Directions:** Place jelly, margarine and lemon juice in 2-quart microwaveproof casserole. Microwave uncovered on high (100%), stirring every minute, until jelly is melted, 3 to 4 minutes. Stir in pineapple and pears. Cover tightly and microwave until fruit is hot, 4 to 5 minutes.

Almond Pilaf

1½ cups uncooked regular rice
1 medium onion, chopped
    (about ½ cup)
¼ cup margarine or butter
½ teaspoon salt
½ teaspoon ground allspice
½ teaspoon ground turmeric

¼ teaspoon curry powder
⅛ teaspoon pepper
1 tablespoon instant chicken
    bouillon
3 cups hot water
¼ cup slivered blanched
    almonds

Cook and stir rice and onion in margarine in 10-inch skillet until onion is tender. Stir in salt, allspice, turmeric, curry powder and pepper; pour into ungreased 2-quart casserole. Stir in instant bouillon and water. Cover and cook in 325° oven until liquid is absorbed and rice is tender, about 40 minutes. Stir in almonds.

Almond-Brown Rice Pilaf: Substitute 1½ cups uncooked brown rice for the regular rice. Cook 60 to 70 minutes.

Spinach-Cucumber Salad

8 ounces spinach, torn into
    bite-size pieces (about
    8 cups)
2 medium cucumbers, thinly
    sliced
½ cup vegetable oil

2 tablespoons sugar
2 tablespoons vinegar
2 teaspoons soy sauce
½ teaspoon dry mustard
¼ teaspoon garlic powder

Place spinach and cucumbers in plastic bag; close tightly and refrigerate no longer than 24 hours. Place remaining ingredients in tightly covered jar and refrigerate. Just before serving, shake dressing; toss with spinach and cucumbers.

Savory Pork Roast

4-pound pork boneless top loin roast	1 teaspoon dried marjoram leaves
1 clove garlic, cut into halves	1 teaspoon salt
1 teaspoon dried sage leaves	

Rub pork roast with cut sides of garlic. Mix remaining ingredients; sprinkle on pork. Place pork fat side up on rack in shallow roasting pan. Insert meat thermometer so tip is in center of thickest part of pork and does not rest in fat. Roast uncovered in 325° oven until meat thermometer registers 170°, 2 to 2½ hours. Garnish with frosted grapes if desired. (To frost grapes, dip in water, then roll in sugar.)

Note: Roasts are easier to carve if allowed to set 15 to 20 minutes after removing from oven. Since meat continues to cook after removal from oven, if roast is to set, it should be removed from oven when thermometer registers 5° lower than desired doneness.

Golden Squash Casserole

6 cups cubed pared Hubbard squash*	1 medium onion, finely chopped
1 cup dairy sour cream	1 teaspoon salt
2 tablespoons margarine or butter	¼ teaspoon pepper

Heat 1 inch salted water (½ teaspoon salt to 1 cup water) to boiling. Add squash. Cover and heat to boiling. Cook until tender, 15 to 20 minutes; drain. Mash squash; stir in remaining ingredients. Turn mixture into ungreased 1-quart casserole. Cook uncovered in 325° oven until hot, 35 to 45 minutes.

*2 packages (12 ounces each) frozen cooked squash, thawed, can be substituted for the cooked fresh squash.

Do-Ahead Tip: Before cooking, casserole can be covered and refrigerated no longer than 24 hours. Cook uncovered in 325° oven until heated through, 50 to 60 minutes.

Mixed Vegetable Medley

1 package (10 ounces) frozen green peas	1 jar (2 ounces) sliced pimiento, drained
1 package (10 ounces) frozen green beans	2 tablespoons margarine or butter
1 package (10 ounces) frozen cauliflower	½ teaspoon dried basil leaves
¾ cup water	½ teaspoon salt
	⅛ teaspoon pepper

Heat vegetables and water to boiling in 3-quart saucepan; reduce heat. Cover and cook over low heat until vegetables are tender, about 7 minutes. Drain; stir in remaining ingredients.

Mandarin Orange Toss

⅓ cup sliced almonds
2 tablespoons sugar
½ head lettuce, torn into
    bite-size pieces
1 small bunch romaine, torn
    into bite-size pieces
2 medium stalks celery, thinly
    sliced (about 1 cup)

2 green onions (with tops),
    thinly sliced (about
    2 tablespoons)
Sweet-Sour Dressing (below)
1 can (11 ounces) mandarin
    orange segments, drained

Cook almonds and sugar over low heat, stirring constantly, until sugar is melted and almonds are coated. Cool and break apart. Store at room temperature. Place lettuce and romaine in plastic bag; add celery and onions. Pour Sweet-Sour Dressing into bag; add orange segments. Close bag tightly and shake until salad greens and orange segments are well coated. Add almonds and shake.

SWEET-SOUR DRESSING

⅓ cup vegetable oil
3 tablespoons sugar
3 tablespoons vinegar
1 tablespoon snipped parsley
    or mint leaves

½ teaspoon salt
    Dash of pepper
    Dash of red pepper sauce

Shake all ingredients in tightly covered jar; refrigerate.

Glazed Baked Ham

Place 5- to 8-pound fully cooked smoked picnic shoulder fat side up on rack in shallow roasting pan. Insert meat thermometer so tip is in thickest part of meat and does not touch bone or rest in fat. Bake uncovered in 325° oven until done, 25 to 30 minutes per pound, or until thermometer registers 140°.

About 30 minutes before ham is done, remove from oven; drain. Cut uniform diamond shapes on fat surface of ham. Insert whole clove in each diamond if desired. Mix ¼ cup honey, ½ teaspoon dry mustard and ¼ teaspoon ground cloves; spoon or spread on ham and bake 30 minutes. Decorate ham with orange slices and maraschino cherries if desired.

Note: Ham is easier to carve if allowed to set 15 to 20 minutes after removing from oven. Since meat continues to cook after removal from oven, if ham is to set, it should be removed from oven when thermometer registers 5° lower than desired temperature.

Cinnamon Sweet Potatoes

2½ pounds sweet potatoes or
    yams (7 or 8 medium)*
½ cup packed brown sugar
¼ cup margarine or butter
3 tablespoons water
½ teaspoon ground cinnamon
½ teaspoon salt

Heat enough salted water to cover potatoes (½ teaspoon salt to 1 cup water) to boiling. Add potatoes. Cover and heat to boiling. Cook until tender, 30 to 35 minutes; drain. Slip off skins. Cut potatoes crosswise into ½-inch slices.

Mix brown sugar, margarine, water, cinnamon and salt in 10-inch skillet. Cook over medium heat, stirring constantly, until smooth. Add potato slices; stir gently until glazed and heated through.

*2 cans (17 ounces each) vacuum-packed sweet potatoes, cut into ½-inch slices, can be substituted for the cooked fresh sweet potatoes.

Orange Sweet Potatoes: Substitute 3 tablespoons orange juice for the water and mix in 1 tablespoon grated orange peel; omit cinnamon.

Tomato-Brussels Sprouts Salad

2 packages (10 ounces each)
    frozen Brussels sprouts
¾ cup oil-and-vinegar salad
    dressing
½ pint cherry tomatoes, cut
    into halves

Cook Brussels sprouts as directed on package. Pour salad dressing over hot Brussels sprouts, turning each until well coated. Cool; cover and refrigerate at least 3 hours. Add tomatoes to Brussels sprouts and toss. Serve in lettuce cups if desired.

Tomato-Brussels Sprouts Salad

Pineapple-Stuffed Spareribs

3-pound rack fresh pork
   spareribs
½ cup chopped celery
1 small onion, chopped
3 tablespoons margarine or
   butter

1 can (15¼ ounces) pineapple
   chunks, drained (reserve
   syrup)
½ teaspoon ground cloves
4 cups packaged seasoned
   stuffing

Tie pork spareribs in circle; place spareribs bone tips up on rack in shallow roasting pan. Do not add water. Roast uncovered in 325° oven 2 hours.

Cook and stir celery and onion in margarine until tender. Mix with pineapple, cloves, stuffing and enough reserved pineapple syrup to moisten. Spoon dressing into circle of spareribs; roast uncovered until spareribs are done, about 30 minutes.

Glazed Carrots

1¼ pounds fresh carrots
   (about 8 medium)
⅓ cup packed brown sugar
2 tablespoons margarine or
   butter

½ teaspoon salt
½ teaspoon grated orange
   peel

Cut carrots crosswise into 2½-inch pieces, then into ⅜-inch strips. Heat 1 inch salted water (½ teaspoon salt to 1 cup water) to boiling. Add carrots. Cover and heat to boiling. Reduce heat and cook until tender, 18 to 20 minutes; drain.

Cook and stir brown sugar, margarine, salt and orange peel in 10-inch skillet until bubbly. Add carrots; cook over low heat, stirring occasionally, until carrots are glazed and heated through, about 5 minutes.

☐ **Microwave Directions:** Mix all ingredients in 1½-quart microwaveproof casserole. Cover tightly and microwave on high (100%), stirring every 3 minutes, until carrots are tender, 9 to 11 minutes.

Spinach-Cauliflower Toss

4 ounces spinach, torn into
   bite-size pieces (about
   4 cups)
¼ small cauliflower, separated
   into flowerets (about
   1 cup)

3 green onions, chopped
4 radishes, sliced
⅓ cup oil-and-vinegar salad
   dressing

Place all ingredients except dressing in plastic bag; refrigerate no longer than 24 hours. Just before serving, shake dressing and pour into bag. Close bag tightly and shake.

MENU

PINEAPPLE-STUFFED SPARERIBS
GLAZED CARROTS
SPINACH-CAULIFLOWER TOSS
SQUASH ROLLS (PAGE 89)
CREAM PUFFS WITH ICE CREAM
(PAGE 72)

4 SERVINGS

Pineapple-Stuffed Spareribs

Herbed Cornish Hens

3 frozen Rock Cornish hens
(about 1 pound each),
thawed
Salt and pepper
¼ cup margarine or butter,
melted

½ teaspoon dried marjoram
leaves
½ teaspoon dried thyme leaves
¼ teaspoon paprika

Rub cavities of hens with salt and pepper. Place hens breast side up on rack in shallow roasting pan. Mix margarine, marjoram, thyme and paprika; brush hens with part of margarine mixture. Roast uncovered in 350° oven, brushing with margarine mixture 5 or 6 times, until done, about 1 hour. To serve, cut each hen into halves with scissors, cutting along backbone from tail to neck and down center of breast. Garnish with watercress if desired.

White and Wild Rice Medley

½ cup slivered almonds
¼ cup uncooked wild rice
1 jar (2½ ounces) sliced
mushrooms, drained
2 tablespoons chopped green
onions

¼ cup margarine or butter
1 tablespoon instant chicken
bouillon
2½ cups boiling water
¾ cup uncooked regular rice

Cook and stir almonds, wild rice, mushrooms and green onions in margarine until almonds are golden brown, 10 to 15 minutes. Pour wild rice mixture into ungreased 1½-quart casserole. Stir in instant bouillon and water. Cover and cook in 350° oven 30 minutes. Stir in regular rice. Cover and cook until liquid is absorbed, about 30 minutes longer.

Asparagus with Pimiento

Cook 2 packages (10 ounces each) frozen asparagus spears as directed on package; drain. Drizzle with lemon juice and melted margarine or butter. Garnish with pimiento strips.

Apple-Grapefruit Salad

Arrange unpared red apple slices and grapefruit sections on salad greens; sprinkle each serving with pomegranate seeds. Serve with Lime-Honey Dressing (below).

LIME-HONEY DRESSING

3 tablespoons frozen limeade
or lemonade concentrate,
thawed

3 tablespoons honey
3 tablespoons vegetable oil
¼ teaspoon poppy seed

Shake all ingredients in tightly covered jar; refrigerate.

Whole Wheat Popovers

4 eggs
2 cups milk
1½ cups all-purpose flour
½ cup whole wheat flour
1 teaspoon salt

Heat oven to 450°. Generously grease twelve 6-ounce custard cups or 16 medium muffin cups, 2½x1¼ inches. Beat eggs slightly; beat in milk, flours and salt just until smooth (do not overbeat).

Fill custard cups about ½ full, muffin cups about ¾ full. Bake 20 minutes. Reduce oven temperature to 350°. Bake until golden brown, 15 to 20 minutes. Immediately remove from cups; serve hot. *12 or 16 popovers.*

Note: Popovers can be reheated on ungreased cookie sheet in 350° oven about 5 minutes. Or wrap in aluminum foil and freeze no longer than 1 month. Remove foil and heat 10 minutes.

MENU

HERBED SALMON STEAKS
DUCHESS POTATOES
GREEN PEAS
AND ARTICHOKE HEARTS
CUCUMBER-PEAR SALAD
DINNER ROLLS
CRANBERRY SUNDAES

4 SERVINGS

Herbed Salmon Steaks

2 tablespoons margarine or
butter
2 tablespoons lemon juice
4 salmon steaks, ¾ inch thick
1 teaspoon onion salt
¼ teaspoon pepper
½ teaspoon dried marjoram or
thyme leaves
Paprika
Lemon wedges
Parsley

Heat margarine and lemon juice in baking dish, 12x7½x2 inches, in 400° oven. Place fish in baking dish; turn to coat both sides with lemon butter. Sprinkle with onion salt, pepper and marjoram leaves. Cook uncovered until fish flakes easily with fork, about 25 minutes. Sprinkle with paprika; serve with lemon wedges and parsley.

Herbed Halibut Steaks: Substitute 4 halibut steaks for the salmon steaks.

Duchess Potatoes

Prepare instant mashed potatoes as directed on package for 4 servings except—decrease milk to 2 tablespoons. In small mixer bowl, beat 1 egg slightly; add hot potatoes and beat on medium speed until fluffy. Drop mixture by spoonfuls (8 to 10) onto greased cookie sheet, or place in pastry tube and form rosettes. Sprinkle with paprika. Bake in 400° oven until golden brown, about 15 minutes.

Green Peas and Artichoke Hearts

1 package (10 ounces) frozen green peas
1 package (10 ounces) frozen artichoke hearts
¾ cup water

1 teaspoon salt
2 tablespoons diced pimiento
1 tablespoon margarine or butter
1 tablespoon lemon juice

Heat vegetables, water and salt to boiling in 2-quart saucepan; reduce heat. Cover and cook until vegetables are tender, 5 to 8 minutes. Drain; stir in remaining ingredients.

Cucumber-Pear Salad

¼ cup vegetable oil
2 tablespoons lemon juice
1 teaspoon sugar
¼ teaspoon salt
Dash of pepper

2 small cucumbers, cut into ¾-inch pieces
2 pears, cut into ¾-inch pieces
Salad greens

Mix oil, lemon juice, sugar, salt and pepper; toss with cucumbers and pears. Refrigerate at least 1 hour. Remove cucumbers and pears with slotted spoon. Serve on salad greens.

Buffets

What's the easiest way to serve dinner to a Christmas crowd? Plan a buffet—it's the ideal way to handle more than the usual number of guests. No matter how formal the food or the setting, there's something wonderfully relaxed about a buffet dinner. If you plan to have your guests seated at the dinner table or card tables, your menu choice is unlimited. But if you're counting on lap, tray or snack-table dining, choose a menu that doesn't require the use of a knife.

Buffet service itself is really a matter of common sense. Arrange the dinner plates at one end of the server, then move on in logical order to the main course, vegetable, salad, bread, condiments and finally the silverware and napkins. If using your dining room table for the buffet, you can set up two serving arrangements, one on each side of the table, to move two lines of guests.

MENU

DILLED MEATBALLS
STROGANOFF

HOT BUTTERED NOODLES

GREEN BEANS WITH RADISHES

MOLDED BEET SALAD

ZUCCHINI TOSS

CRUSTY ROLLS

LIME MERINGUE DESSERT
(PAGE 63)

12 SERVINGS

Dilled Meatballs Stroganoff

Meatballs (below)	1 cup milk
3 cans (10¾ ounces each) condensed cream of chicken soup	1 teaspoon dried dill weed
	1½ cups dairy sour cream
	Snipped parsley

Prepare meatballs. Mix soup, milk and dill weed in Dutch oven; add meatballs. Heat to boiling, stirring occasionally; reduce heat. Cover and simmer 15 minutes. Stir in sour cream; heat through. Sprinkle with parsley.

MEATBALLS

3 pounds ground beef	1 tablespoon salt
1½ cups dry bread crumbs	1½ teaspoons Worcestershire sauce
¾ cup milk	
3 eggs	¼ teaspoon pepper
1 small onion, finely chopped	

Mix all ingredients. Shape ⅓ of meat mixture by level tablespoonfuls into 1-inch balls. Place in ungreased jelly roll pan, 15½x10½x1 inch. Cook in 400° oven until light brown, 18 to 20 minutes. Repeat with remaining meat mixture. *About 8 dozen meatballs.*

Do-Ahead Tip: Meatballs can be prepared ahead of time and frozen. Cool 5 minutes after cooking; drain. Freeze uncovered 15 minutes. Place meatballs in freezer containers. Cover, label and freeze no longer than 2 months. Add frozen meatballs to soup mixture (above). Cover and simmer, stirring occasionally, until meatballs are hot, 50 to 60 minutes.

Hot Buttered Noodles

Cook 14 to 16 ounces wide egg noodles as directed on package. Drain quickly in colander or sieve. Toss with ¼ cup margarine or butter; this will keep noodles separated. (If desired, cook and stir ½ cup chopped green pepper and ¼ cup chopped onion in the margarine until onion is tender; stir into noodles.)

Green Beans with Radishes

3 packages (9 ounces each) frozen cut green beans	8 radishes, thinly sliced
¾ cup water	½ teaspoon salt
2 tablespoons margarine or butter	⅛ teaspoon pepper

Heat beans and water to boiling in 3-quart saucepan; reduce heat. Cover and simmer, stirring occasionally, until tender, about 10 minutes; drain. Toss beans with margarine, radishes, salt and pepper.

Molded Beet Salad

1 can (16 ounces) shoestring beets, drained (reserve liquid)	¼ cup vinegar
1 package (6 ounces) lemon-flavored gelatin	⅛ teaspoon salt
1 cup cold water	1 cup finely chopped celery
¼ cup sugar	2 tablespoons finely chopped onion
	Salad greens

Add enough water to reserved beet liquid to measure 2½ cups; heat to boiling. Pour on gelatin in bowl; stir until gelatin is dissolved. Stir in cold water, sugar, vinegar and salt. Refrigerate until slightly thickened but not set. Fold in beets, celery and onion. Pour into 6-cup mold. Refrigerate until firm. Unmold on salad greens.

Zucchini Toss

1 medium bunch romaine, torn into pieces	4 green onions, sliced
3 tablespoons olive or vegetable oil	1½ tablespoons tarragon or wine vinegar
2 small zucchini, sliced	½ teaspoon salt
1 cup cherry tomatoes, cut into halves	1 small clove garlic, crushed
	Dash of freshly ground pepper

Toss romaine and oil until leaves glisten. Add remaining ingredients; toss.

Green Beans with Radishes

Buffet Ham

MENU

BUFFET HAM
PARTY POTATO CASSEROLE
VEGETABLE BUFFET PLATTER
CUCUMBER-LIME MOLD
CLOVERLEAF ROLLS (PAGE 88)
CHERRY-BERRIES ON A CLOUD
(PAGE 63)

12 SERVINGS

4½- to 5-pound fully cooked
   boneless smoked ham,
   cut into ¼-inch slices
   and tied
3 tablespoons corn syrup

2 tablespoons brown sugar
1 teaspoon prepared mustard
   Mustard Sauce and Raisin
   Sauce (below)

Place ham on rack in shallow roasting pan. Heat in 325° oven until hot, 1 to 1¼ hours. Mix corn syrup, brown sugar and mustard; brush on ham during last 15 minutes of heating. Garnish with apricot halves and parsley if desired. Serve with sauces.

MUSTARD SAUCE

1 tablespoon margarine or
   butter
1 tablespoon flour
½ teaspoon salt
¼ teaspoon pepper

1 cup milk
3 tablespoons prepared
   mustard
1 tablespoon prepared
   horseradish

Heat margarine over low heat until melted. Blend in flour, salt and pepper. Cook over low heat, stirring constantly, until smooth and bubbly; remove from heat. Stir in milk. Heat to boiling, stirring constantly. Boil and stir 1 minute. Stir in mustard and horseradish. Heat until hot; cool.   *About 1¼ cups sauce.*

RAISIN SAUCE

½ cup packed brown sugar
2 tablespoons cornstarch
1 teaspoon dry mustard

1¼ cups water
2 tablespoons lemon juice
1 cup raisins

Mix brown sugar, cornstarch and mustard in 1-quart saucepan. Gradually stir in water and lemon juice; add raisins. Cook over medium heat, stirring constantly, until mixture boils. Boil and stir 1 minute.   *About 1½ cups sauce.*

Party Potato Casserole

2 cans (10¾ ounces each)
   cream of celery soup
1 carton (8 ounces) dairy sour
   cream or unflavored yogurt
1 medium onion, chopped
1 green pepper, chopped

3 tablespoons diced pimiento
2 teaspoons salt
⅛ teaspoon pepper
1 bag (32 ounces) frozen hash
   brown potatoes*
¼ cup grated Parmesan cheese

Mix all ingredients except potatoes and Parmesan cheese. Stir in potatoes. Spread in ungreased baking dish, 13x9x2 inches, or 3-quart casserole. Sprinkle with Parmesan cheese. Cover and cook in 325° oven 1 hour. Uncover and cook until potatoes are tender, about 30 minutes. Sprinkle with paprika if desired.

*8 cups cubed potatoes (about 8 medium) can be substituted for the frozen potatoes.

Do-Ahead Tip: Before cooking, casserole can be covered and refrigerated no longer than 24 hours.

Vegetable Buffet Platter

¼ large head red cabbage, shredded (about 3 cups)
8 ounces broccoli, cut into bite-size pieces (about 2 cups)
4 medium carrots, shredded (about 2 cups)
4 medium stalks celery, thinly sliced (about 2 cups)
1 medium jicama or 1 small rutabaga, cut into sticks, 3x¼ inch (about 2 cups)

½ small cauliflower, separated into tiny flowerets (about 2 cups)
Pitted ripe olives
Buttermilk Dressing (below), Blue Cheese Dressing (page 161) and Ruby French Dressing (page 161)

Arrange vegetables in separate sections on platter; garnish with ripe olives. Serve with choice of dressings.

BUTTERMILK DRESSING

¾ cup mayonnaise or salad dressing
½ cup buttermilk
1 teaspoon dried parsley flakes

½ teaspoon instant minced onion
1 clove garlic, crushed
½ teaspoon salt
Dash of ground pepper

Shake all ingredients in tightly covered jar; refrigerate at least 2 hours. Shake before serving.   *1¼ cups dressing*.

Cucumber-Lime Mold

1 cup boiling water
2 packages (3 ounces each) lime-flavored gelatin
¾ cup cold water
1 cup boiling water
½ cup mayonnaise or salad dressing
¼ cup cold water

2 tablespoons vinegar
¼ teaspoon salt
1 medium cucumber, chopped (about 1 cup)
1 medium stalk celery, chopped (about ½ cup)
7 medium radishes, sliced (about ½ cup)

For first layer, pour 1 cup boiling water on 1 package gelatin in bowl; stir until gelatin is dissolved. Stir in ¾ cup cold water. Pour ½ cup of the gelatin mixture into 5-cup mold; refrigerate. Reserve remaining gelatin mixture for third layer.

For second layer, pour 1 cup boiling water on second package gelatin in bowl; stir until gelatin is dissolved. Mix mayonnaise, ¼ cup cold water, the vinegar and salt; stir into gelatin mixture. Refrigerate until slightly thickened, about 1 hour. Stir in half of the cucumber, celery and radishes. Pour on the first layer in mold; refrigerate.

For third layer, refrigerate reserved gelatin until slightly thickened, about 1 hour. Stir in remaining vegetables; pour on second layer in mold. Refrigerate until firm, at least 5 hours.

Lasagne

- 1 pound bulk Italian sausage or ground beef
- 1 medium onion, chopped (about ½ cup)
- 1 clove garlic, pressed
- 1 can (16 ounces) whole tomatoes
- 1 can (15 ounces) tomato sauce
- 2 tablespoons dried parsley flakes
- 1 teaspoon sugar
- 1 teaspoon dried basil leaves
- ½ teaspoon salt
- 9 uncooked lasagne noodles (about 8 ounces)

- 1 carton (16 ounces) ricotta or creamed cottage cheese (about 2 cups)
- ¼ cup grated Parmesan cheese
- 1 tablespoon dried parsley flakes
- 1½ teaspoons salt
- 1½ teaspoons dried oregano leaves
- 2 cups shredded mozzarella cheese (about 8 ounces)
- ¼ cup grated Parmesan cheese

Cook and stir Italian sausage, onion and garlic in 10-inch skillet until sausage is light brown; drain. Add tomatoes (with liquid), tomato sauce, 2 tablespoons parsley, the sugar, basil and ½ teaspoon salt. Heat to boiling, stirring occasionally; reduce heat. Simmer uncovered until mixture is consistency of thick spaghetti sauce, about 1 hour.

Cook noodles as directed on package. Reserve ½ cup of the sauce mixture. Mix ricotta cheese, ¼ cup Parmesan cheese, 1 tablespoon parsley, 1½ teaspoons salt and the oregano. Layer ⅓ each of the noodles, remaining sauce mixture, mozzarella cheese and ricotta cheese mixture in ungreased baking pan, 13x9x2 inches. Repeat 2 times. Spoon reserved sauce mixture onto top; sprinkle with ¼ cup Parmesan cheese. Cook uncovered in 350° oven 45 minutes. Let stand 15 minutes before cutting.

Do-Ahead Tip: After cooking, lasagne can be covered and frozen no longer than 3 weeks. To serve, cook uncovered in 375° oven until bubbly, about 1 hour.

Antipasto Toss

- 1 can (15 ounces) garbanzo beans, drained
- 1 jar (about 6 ounces) marinated artichoke hearts
- ½ cup pitted ripe olives, cut into halves
- ½ cup herb-and-garlic or Italian salad dressing

- 2 bunches romaine, torn into bite-size pieces
- 1 bunch leaf lettuce, torn into bite-size pieces
- ½ cup sliced pepperoni, if desired
  Freshly ground pepper

Toss beans, artichoke hearts (with liquid), olives and salad dressing. Cover and refrigerate. Just before serving, toss with remaining ingredients.

MENU

LASAGNE
ANTIPASTO TOSS
VEGETABLE RELISHES
BREAD STICKS
CHRISTMAS TORTONI (PAGE 64)
ESPRESSO

8 TO 10 SERVINGS

Antipasto Toss (directions for the Della Robbia Wreath Candle Holder are on page 187)

Turkey Curry

Condiments (below)
2 medium onions, chopped
2 medium stalks celery,
  chopped
½ cup margarine or butter
½ cup all-purpose flour
3 to 4 teaspoons curry powder
½ teaspoon garlic salt
½ teaspoon salt
¼ to ½ teaspoon ground
  cinnamon

¼ teaspoon pepper
3 cups water
1 tablespoon instant chicken
  bouillon
1 can (4 ounces) mushroom
  stems and pieces
1 cup half-and-half or milk
4 cups cut-up cooked turkey

Prepare 4 to 6 of the Condiments. Cook and stir onions and celery in margarine in Dutch oven until onion is tender. Blend in flour, curry powder, garlic salt, salt, cinnamon and pepper. Cook over low heat, stirring constantly, until mixture is hot and bubbly; remove from heat. Stir in water and instant bouillon. Heat to boiling, stirring constantly. Boil and stir 1 minute. Stir in mushrooms (with liquid), half-and-half and turkey. Serve with Condiments.

CONDIMENTS
Chopped hard-cooked egg, crumbled crisp bacon, chutney, raisins, pineapple chunks, chopped preserved ginger, chopped green pepper, chopped salted peanuts.

Cucumber-Tomato Yogurt

2 medium cucumbers
2 medium tomatoes, chopped
2 green onions (with tops),
  chopped
1 tablespoon snipped parsley

1 carton (8 ounces) unflavored
  yogurt (1 cup)
½ teaspoon salt
¼ teaspoon ground cumin

Cut cucumbers lengthwise into halves. Scoop out seeds and cut cucumbers into ½-inch pieces. Mix cucumbers, tomatoes, onions and parsley; cover and refrigerate. Mix yogurt, salt and cumin; cover and refrigerate. At serving time, drain vegetables and fold into yogurt dressing. Garnish with additional chopped cucumbers and tomatoes if desired.

Parsleyed Rice

Heat 2⅔ cups rice, 5⅓ cups water and 2 teaspoons salt to boiling in 3-quart saucepan, stirring once or twice; reduce heat. Cover and simmer 14 minutes. (Do not lift cover or stir.) Remove from heat. Fluff rice lightly with fork; cover and let steam 5 to 10 minutes. Stir in ¼ cup snipped parsley. If a rice ring is desired, press lightly in well-greased 6½-cup ring mold. Keep hot until serving time. Invert on warm serving plate.

Spinach Salad with Sesame Seed Dressing

Place 16 ounces spinach, torn into bite-size pieces, in plastic bag; close bag and refrigerate. Just before serving, toss with Sesame Seed Dressing (below).

SESAME SEED DRESSING
Mix ½ cup oil-and-vinegar salad dressing, 1 tablespoon toasted sesame seed* and ¼ teaspoon dried basil leaves.

*To toast sesame seed, heat in 6-inch skillet, stirring occasionally, until golden brown.

Almond Flatbread

¾ cup toasted almonds	2 tablespoons margarine or
1 cup all-purpose flour	butter, softened
1½ teaspoons sugar	¼ cup dairy sour cream
½ teaspoon salt	3 tablespoons milk
¼ teaspoon baking soda	

Heat oven to 400°. Grind nuts in blender, watching carefully (nuts can be finely chopped by hand). Mix all ingredients with fork. Pinch off 1-inch balls. Roll each ball into 4-inch circle on floured surface. Bake on ungreased cookie sheet until golden brown, 6 to 8 minutes.   *About 2½ dozen rounds.*

Turkey-Wild Rice Casserole

½ cup margarine or butter
½ cup all-purpose flour
2 teaspoons salt
¼ teaspoon pepper
1½ cups chicken broth
2¼ cups milk
 Cooked White and Wild
 Rice (below)
3 cups cut-up cooked turkey
 or chicken (see note)

2 cans (4 ounces each)
 mushroom stems and
 pieces, drained
½ cup chopped green pepper
1 jar (2 ounces) sliced
 pimiento, drained
⅓ cup slivered almonds

Heat margarine in Dutch oven until melted. Blend in flour, salt and pepper. Cook over low heat, stirring constantly, until smooth and bubbly; remove from heat. Stir in chicken broth and milk. Heat to boiling, stirring constantly. Boil and stir 1 minute. Stir in remaining ingredients. Pour into ungreased baking dish, 13x9x2 inches. Cook uncovered in 350° oven until hot and bubbly, 40 to 45 minutes. Sprinkle with snipped parsley if desired.

COOKED WHITE AND WILD RICE
Wash ½ cup wild rice. Heat wild rice, 1¼ cups water and 1 teaspoon salt in 2-quart saucepan to boiling; reduce heat. Cover and simmer 30 minutes. Add ½ cup regular white rice and 1 cup water. Heat to boiling; reduce heat. Cover and simmer 15 minutes. Remove from heat. Fluff rice with fork; cover and let stand 5 minutes.   *About 3 cups cooked rice.*

Do-Ahead Tip: Before cooking, casserole can be covered and refrigerated no longer than 24 hours.

Note: An easy way to cook turkey for leftovers is poaching. Cut turkey into fourths; place in large kettle with enough water to cover bottom of kettle. Sprinkle with 2 tablespoons salt and 2 teaspoons white pepper. Heat to boiling; reduce heat. Cover and simmer until turkey is done, 2 to 2½ hours. Remove turkey from broth; cover and refrigerate at least 1 hour but no longer than 2 days. Remove meat from bones and cut up. A 5- to 6-pound turkey roast will yield 10 to 12 cups meat; a 12-pound turkey, 14 cups.

Cranberry-Pineapple Salad

1 can (16 ounces) jellied
 cranberry sauce, cut into 12
 slices
3 cans (8¼ ounces each) sliced
 pineapple, drained

Salad greens
Mayonnaise or salad
 dressing

Arrange cranberry and pineapple slices on salad greens. Serve with mayonnaise.

Brunches

Informal entertaining at its best—that's brunch. And a festive brunch is particularly well suited to the Christmas season, for with so many people on vacation, there's no need to relegate it to the weekend. Following are three light and easy menus to brighten up any morning. (They'd be fine, too, for luncheons or late-night suppers.) Prepare everything you can in advance, then let the main dish bake while you greet your guests. Easy does it!

Sparkling Red Rouser

Just before serving, mix 2 bottles (7 ounces each) lemon-lime carbonated beverage (about 2 cups) and 1 can (8 ounces) tomato sauce. Serve over ice. Allow about ½ cup for each serving.

Crab Quiche

 4 eggs
1½ cups dairy sour cream
 ½ cup grated Parmesan
    cheese
 ¼ cup all-purpose flour
 1 teaspoon onion powder
 ¼ teaspoon salt

 4 drops red pepper sauce
 1 can (6½ ounces) crabmeat,
    drained
 1 can (4 ounces) mushroom
    stems and pieces, drained
 2 cups shredded Swiss cheese
    (about 8 ounces)

Mix eggs, sour cream, Parmesan cheese, flour, onion powder, salt and pepper sauce in 4-quart bowl; beat with hand beater until smooth. Stir in crabmeat, mushrooms and Swiss cheese. Pour into ungreased 10-inch pie plate. Cook in 350° oven until knife inserted near center comes out clean, about 45 minutes. Cool 5 minutes before serving.

Winter Fruit Salad

4 oranges or 2 grapefruit
1 ripe avocado
1 large red apple, sliced
   Lemon juice

   Spinach leaves
 ½ cup whole cranberry sauce
   Lime-Honey Dressing
   (page 112)

Pare and section oranges. Cut avocado lengthwise into ¼-inch slices. Sprinkle avocado and apple slices with lemon juice. Arrange orange, avocado and apple slices on spinach. Spoon cranberry sauce into center. Serve with Lime-Honey Dressing.

MENU

SPARKLING RED ROUSER
CRAB QUICHE
WINTER FRUIT SALAD
CRESCENT ROLLS (PAGE 88)

6 TO 8 SERVINGS

Mixed Fruit Medley

½ cup orange-flavored liqueur
4 cups cut-up fresh pineapple
2 cups seedless green grapes,
  halved

2 cups fresh strawberries or 1
  package (12 ounces) frozen
  whole strawberries,
  partially thawed

Pour orange-flavored liqueur on pineapple and green grapes; toss. Just before serving, stir in strawberries. Garnish with mint leaves if desired.

Easy Oven Omelet

¼ cup margarine or butter
18 eggs
1 cup dairy sour cream
1 cup milk
2 teaspoons salt
¼ teaspoon dried basil leaves
2 cups shredded Cheddar or
  American process cheese
  (8 ounces)

1 can (4 ounces) mushroom
  stems and pieces, drained
4 green onions (with tops),
  thinly sliced (about
  ¼ cup)
1 jar (2 ounces) diced
  pimiento, drained

Heat margarine in baking dish, 13x9x2 inches, in 325° oven until melted. Tilt dish to coat bottom with margarine. Beat eggs, sour cream, milk, salt and basil in large mixer bowl until blended. Stir in cheese, mushrooms, green onions and pimiento. Pour into baking dish. Cook uncovered until omelet is set but still moist, 40 to 45 minutes. Cut omelet into twelve 3-inch squares. Garnish with sliced green onion tops if desired.

Do-Ahead Tip: After pouring into baking dish, cover and refrigerate no longer than 24 hours. Cook uncovered in 325° oven 50 to 55 minutes.

Festive Egg Squares

1 pound bulk pork sausage,
  cooked and drained
4 ounces mushrooms, sliced
½ cup sliced green onions
  (with tops)
2 medium tomatoes, chopped
2 cups shredded mozzarella
  cheese (about 8 ounces)

1¼ cups buttermilk baking mix
12 eggs
1 cup milk
1½ teaspoons salt
½ teaspoon pepper
½ teaspoon dried oregano
  leaves

Layer sausage, mushrooms, green onions, tomatoes and cheese in greased baking dish, 13x9x2 inches. Beat remaining ingredients; pour over sausage mixture. Cook uncovered in 350° oven until golden brown and set, about 30 minutes. Cut into twelve 3-inch squares.

Catawba Fruit Cup

Thaw 3 packages (10 ounces each) frozen mixed fruit as directed on packages; do not drain. Spoon about ⅓ cup fruit with syrup into each of 8 sherbet dishes. Pour about ¼ cup pink sparkling catawba grape juice into each dish; stir once. Serve immediately.

Ham-Cheese Omelet Roll

¼ cup margarine or butter
½ cup all-purpose flour
2 cups milk
4 egg yolks
½ teaspoon salt
  Dash of ground red pepper
2 teaspoons snipped chives
4 egg whites
¼ teaspoon cream of tartar

⅓ cup grated Parmesan
  cheese
  Cheese Sauce (below)
1½ cups finely chopped fully
  cooked smoked ham
2 tablespoons snipped
  parsley
½ cup milk

Grease jelly roll pan, 15½x10½x1 inch. Line bottom of pan with waxed paper; grease lightly and flour. Heat margarine over medium heat until melted. Remove from heat; stir in flour. Cook over low heat, stirring constantly, until smooth and bubbly. Remove from heat; stir in 2 cups milk. Heat to boiling, stirring constantly. Boil and stir 1 minute. Remove from heat. Beat in egg yolks, one at a time. Stir in salt, red pepper and chives. Cool at room temperature, stirring occasionally. (Cover mixture to prevent formation of film.)

Heat oven to 350°. Beat egg whites and cream of tartar in large mixer bowl until stiff but not dry. Stir about ¼ of the egg whites into egg yolk mixture. Gently fold egg yolk mixture and Parmesan cheese into remaining egg whites. Pour into pan. Bake until puffed and golden brown, about 45 minutes.

While omelet is baking, prepare Cheese Sauce; keep warm. Stir ham and parsley into 1 cup of the sauce. Immediately loosen omelet from edges of pan; invert on cloth-covered rack. Spread omelet with ham mixture; roll up from narrow end. Stir ½ cup milk into remaining sauce; heat. Pour part of sauce over roll; serve remaining sauce separately. Sprinkle roll with snipped parsley if desired.

CHEESE SAUCE

1 small onion, finely chopped
3 tablespoons margarine or
  butter
3 tablespoons flour
1 teaspoon dry mustard

  Dash of pepper
1½ cups milk
1 cup shredded Swiss cheese
5 drops red pepper sauce

Cook and stir onion in margarine in saucepan until onion is tender. Blend in flour, mustard and pepper. Cook over low heat, stirring constantly, until mixture is smooth and bubbly. Stir in milk. Heat to boiling, stirring constantly. Boil and stir 1 minute. Add cheese and pepper sauce; stir until cheese is melted.

Ham-Cheese Omelet Roll

Holiday Suppers

For many families, Christmas Eve has just as many traditions as Christmas Day. Some families open gifts and round out the evening with a midnight supper, others have a special supper before evening church services, still others share the evening with friends. The following menus feature do-ahead casseroles and a choice of hearty soups—they're simple but sophisticated, perfect for any of these plans.

Shrimp-Rice Casserole

3 cups cooked rice
1 small onion, chopped (about ¼ cup)
¼ cup snipped parsley
1 jar (2 ounces) diced pimiento, drained
1 cup shredded sharp Cheddar cheese (about 4 ounces)
1 teaspoon salt
1 teaspoon Worcestershire sauce
1 package (6 ounces) frozen tiny shrimp
3 eggs, slightly beaten
2 cups milk
  Shrimp Sauce (below)
1 lime, cut into eighths

Mix all ingredients except Shrimp Sauce and lime in ungreased baking dish, 13x9x2 inches. Cook uncovered in 325° oven until knife inserted in center comes out clean, about 45 minutes. Cut into squares; serve with Shrimp Sauce and lime.

SHRIMP SAUCE

1 can (10¾ ounces) condensed cream of shrimp soup
½ cup dairy sour cream
1 teaspoon lemon juice
¼ teaspoon salt
2 drops red pepper sauce

Heat all ingredients, stirring constantly, just until hot.

Do-Ahead Tip: Before cooking, cover and refrigerate no longer than 24 hours. To serve, cook uncovered 50 to 60 minutes.

Avocado-Apple Salad

2 ripe avocados
1 large red apple, sliced
  Lemon juice
  Endive
  Pomegranate seeds
  Fruit salad dressing

Cut avocados lengthwise into ¼-inch slices. Sprinkle avocado and apple slices with lemon juice. Arrange avocado and apple slices on endive. Sprinkle with pomegranate seeds; drizzle with dressing.

MENU

SHRIMP-RICE CASSEROLE
AVOCADO-APPLE SALAD
YAM MUFFINS (PAGE 96)
BÛCHE DE NOËL (PAGE 48)

8 SERVINGS

Vegetable-Cheese Soup

2 large potatoes, finely chopped
2 large onions, finely chopped
½ cup finely chopped carrots
½ cup finely chopped celery
2 cans (12 ounces each) beer or 3 cups water
4 teaspoons instant chicken bouillon
2 cups shredded Cheddar or process American cheese (about 8 ounces)
1 cup half-and-half
6 drops red pepper sauce
⅛ teaspoon ground nutmeg
¼ cup snipped parsley

Heat vegetables, beer and instant bouillon to boiling in 3-quart saucepan; reduce heat. Cover and simmer until vegetables are tender, about 15 minutes. Stir in remaining ingredients except parsley; heat through. Sprinkle with parsley.

Oyster Stew

⅓ cup margarine or butter
1½ pints fresh oysters
3 cups milk
¾ cup half-and-half
1 teaspoon salt
Dash of pepper

Heat margarine in 2-quart saucepan until melted. Add oysters (with liquid). Cook and stir over low heat just until edges curl. Heat milk and half-and-half in 3-quart saucepan. Stir in salt, pepper and oysters.

Cherry Ribbon Salad

1¼ cups boiling water
1 package (3 ounces) cherry-flavored gelatin
1 can (21 ounces) cherry pie filling
1 cup boiling water
1 package (3 ounces) orange-pineapple–flavored gelatin
1 can (8¼ ounces) crushed pineapple
⅓ cup mayonnaise or salad dressing
1 cup frozen whipped topping (thawed)
¼ cup chopped pecans, if desired
Salad greens

Pour 1¼ cups boiling water on cherry-flavored gelatin in bowl; stir until gelatin is dissolved. Stir in pie filling. Pour into 6½-cup mold or baking dish, 11x7x1½ inches. Refrigerate until firm, about 1 hour. Pour 1 cup boiling water on orange-pineapple–flavored gelatin in bowl; stir until gelatin is dissolved. Stir in pineapple (with syrup). Refrigerate until slightly thickened but not set, about 30 minutes. Mix mayonnaise and whipped topping. Gradually stir pineapple mixture into mayonnaise mixture. Stir in pecans; pour over cherry layer. Refrigerate until firm. Unmold on plate. Garnish with salad greens.

Strawberry Ribbon Salad: Substitute 1 package (16 ounces) frozen strawberries for the pie filling; stir until strawberries are thawed.

Crunchy Beef-Noodle Casserole

1 pound ground beef	2 teaspoons Worcestershire
1 large onion, chopped	sauce
1 can (10¾ ounces) condensed	⅛ teaspoon pepper
cream of chicken soup	5 ounces egg noodles, cooked
1 can (4 ounces) mushroom	and drained
stems and pieces	1 cup shredded sharp
¾ cup milk	Cheddar or process
1 small green pepper,	American cheese (about
chopped	4 ounces)
½ cup sliced pitted ripe olives	1 cup chow mein noodles
2 tablespoons soy sauce	½ cup mixed salted nuts

Cook and stir ground beef and onion in 10-inch skillet until beef is light brown; drain. Stir in soup, mushrooms (with liquid), milk, green pepper, olives, soy sauce, Worcestershire sauce, pepper and egg noodles. Pour into ungreased 2-quart casserole; sprinkle with cheese. Cover and cook in 350° oven 50 minutes. Top with chow mein noodles and nuts. Cook uncovered 10 minutes.

Do-Ahead Tip: After sprinkling with cheese, casserole can be covered and refrigerated no longer than 24 hours.

Christmas Eve Fruit Salad

1 can (11 ounces) mandarin	1 tablespoon lemon juice
orange segments, drained	Shredded lettuce
1 can (8¼ ounces) sliced beets,	1 tablespoon sugar
drained	¼ cup chopped peanuts
1 can (8¼ ounces) pineapple	¼ cup mayonnaise or salad
chunks	dressing
2 tart red apples, cut up	2 tablespoons milk
1 banana, sliced	

Place orange segments, beets, pineapple (with syrup), apples and banana in bowl. Add lemon juice; toss gently. Let stand 10 minutes; drain. Arrange mixture on platter of shredded lettuce. Sprinkle with sugar and peanuts. Mix mayonnaise and milk; drizzle over fruit.

Garlic French Bread

Cut half of a 1-pound loaf French bread horizontally into halves. Mix ¼ cup margarine or butter, softened, and ⅛ teaspoon garlic powder; spread mixture generously on cut sides of loaf. Reassemble loaf; cut crosswise into 2-inch slices. Wrap loaf securely in aluminum foil. Heat in 350° oven 15 to 20 minutes.   *12 to 14 slices.*

Busy-Day Dinners

These quick and easy dinners were designed to lighten your load on those never-enough-time days during the holiday season. They're fast enough for family, but festive enough for friends. And don't miss the menus featuring cooked turkey and ham—they're guaranteed to take the groan out of left-overs. With meals like these, no one will know what a hectic day you've had.

Yorkshire Beef

MENU

YORKSHIRE BEEF

LEMON-GLAZED BEETS

LETTUCE WEDGES
WITH BLUE CHEESE DRESSING
(PAGE 161)

BUTTERSCOTCH MERINGUE
CAKE (PAGE 57)

6 SERVINGS

1 pound ground beef
1 can (15 ounces) tomato
  sauce
¼ cup chopped green pepper
2 tablespoons flour
1 teaspoon dried parsley
  flakes
½ teaspoon salt
¼ teaspoon pepper
1 cup shredded Cheddar
  cheese (about 4 ounces)
2 eggs
1 cup milk
1 tablespoon vegetable oil
1 cup all-purpose flour
½ teaspoon salt
2 tablespoons chopped green
  onions

Heat oven to 425°. Cook and stir ground beef in 10-inch skillet until brown; drain. Stir in tomato sauce, green pepper, 2 tablespoons flour, the parsley flakes, ½ teaspoon salt and the pepper. Heat to boiling, stirring constantly. Boil and stir 1 minute. Pour into ungreased baking pan, 13x9x2 inches. Sprinkle cheese on top.

Beat eggs, milk, oil, 1 cup flour and ½ teaspoon salt with hand beater until smooth; pour over cheese. Sprinkle with green onions. Bake until golden brown, 25 to 30 minutes. Serve immediately.

Lemon-Glazed Beets

Mix ⅓ cup lemon or orange marmalade and 1 tablespoon vinegar in 2-quart saucepan. Stir in 2 cans (16 ounces each) sliced beets, drained. Cover and heat just until beets are hot, about 10 minutes.

☐ **Microwave Directions:** Mix marmalade and vinegar in 1½-quart microwaveproof casserole; stir in beets. Cover tightly and microwave on high (100%) until hot, 4 to 6 minutes, stirring once.

Beef-Taco Casserole

1 pound ground beef
1 medium onion, chopped
1 can (15½ ounces) kidney
   beans
1 can (8 ounces) tomato sauce
2 teaspoons chili powder

½ teaspoon garlic salt
1 cup broken tortilla chips
1 cup shredded Cheddar or
   process American cheese
   (about 4 ounces)

Cook and stir ground beef and onion in 10-inch skillet until beef is light brown; drain. Stir in kidney beans (with liquid), tomato sauce, chili powder and garlic salt. Heat to boiling. Pour half of the meat mixture into ungreased 1½-quart casserole; top with tortilla chips. Pour remaining beef mixture on top; sprinkle with cheese. Cover and cook in 350° oven until bubbly, 25 to 30 minutes. Garnish with chopped green pepper and pimiento if desired.

Orange-Avocado Salad

3 oranges, pared and sliced
1 avocado, cut into wedges
1 small onion, sliced and
   separated into rings

Salad greens
Orange Dressing (below)

Arrange orange slices, avocado wedges and onion rings on salad greens. Drizzle Orange Dressing on salads.

ORANGE DRESSING

½ cup vegetable oil
2 tablespoons lemon juice
1 teaspoon grated orange peel
¼ cup orange juice

1 tablespoon sugar
¼ teaspoon salt
¼ teaspoon dry mustard

Shake all ingredients in tightly covered jar.

Mexican Chocolate

1½ ounces unsweetened
   chocolate
¼ cup sugar
1 tablespoon plus 2
   teaspoons instant coffee
½ teaspoon ground
   cinnamon

¼ teaspoon ground nutmeg
Dash of salt
¾ cup water
2 cups milk
Whipped cream

Heat chocolate, sugar, coffee, cinnamon, nutmeg, salt and water in 1½-quart saucepan over low heat, stirring constantly, until chocolate is melted and mixture is smooth. Heat to boiling; reduce heat. Simmer uncovered, stirring constantly, 4 minutes. Stir in milk; heat through. Just before serving, beat with hand beater until foamy. Top each serving with whipped cream.

Turkey Divan Casserole

1 bag (16 ounces) frozen
   cut-up broccoli
1 tablespoon lemon juice
3 cups cut-up cooked turkey or
   chicken
6 slices process American
   cheese

1 can (10¾ ounces) condensed
   cream of chicken soup
½ cup milk
1 can (3 ounces) French fried
   onion rings

Spread broccoli in ungreased baking dish, 12x7½x2 inches; drizzle with lemon juice. Top with turkey and cheese slices. Mix soup and milk; pour over turkey and cheese. Cook uncovered in 350° oven until hot and bubbly, about 30 minutes. Sprinkle with onion rings; cook 5 minutes longer.

MENU

TURKEY DIVAN CASSEROLE
PINEAPPLE-TOMATO SALAD
PUMPKIN MUFFINS (PAGE 96)
CHOCOLATE SUNDAES

8 SERVINGS

Pineapple-Tomato Salad

2 cans (8¼ ounces each) sliced
   pineapple, drained
8 green pepper rings
2 tomatoes, sliced

Salad greens
Sweet-Sour Dressing
  (page 109)

Arrange pineapple slices, green pepper rings and tomato slices on salad greens. Serve with Sweet-Sour Dressing.

Ham Loaf Superb

1 pound ground ham (about 3½ cups)	1 small onion, finely chopped
½ pound ground beef	1 teaspoon salt
½ pound ground lean pork	¼ teaspoon pepper
2 eggs, beaten	4 square slices mozzarella, American or Swiss cheese, cut diagonally into triangles
1 cup quick-cooking oats	
¾ cup tomato juice	

Mix all ingredients except cheese. Shape mixture into loaf, 8x4x3 inches, in ungreased baking pan, 13x9x2 inches. Cook uncovered in 350° oven until done, 1 to 1¼ hours. Remove from oven; let stand a few minutes. Transfer ham loaf to ovenproof platter. Make slits about ⅓ of the way through loaf at 1-inch intervals; place a cheese triangle long side down in each. Place loaf in oven until cheese is slightly melted, 2 to 3 minutes.

Hot Mustard Fruit

2 tablespoons packed brown sugar	1 teaspoon prepared mustard
1 tablespoon margarine or butter	1 can (17 ounces) mixed fruit for salads, drained
	1 banana, cut into 1-inch slices

Mix brown sugar, margarine and mustard; reserve 1 tablespoon for topping. Toss remaining mustard mixture with fruit; pour into 1-quart casserole. Spoon reserved mustard mixture over top. Cook uncovered in 350° oven 20 minutes.

Baked Sweet Potatoes

Scrub 6 to 8 medium sweet potatoes or yams and, if desired, rub with small amount shortening for softer skins. Prick with fork to allow steam to escape. Cook in 350° oven until soft, about 50 minutes.

To serve, cut crisscross gashes in each potato; squeeze gently until some potato pops up through opening. Dot with margarine and sprinkle with salt and pepper.

Green Peas with Celery and Onion

2 packages (10 ounces each) frozen green peas	3 tablespoons margarine or butter, softened
½ cup sliced celery	¼ teaspoon salt
1 small onion, thinly sliced	

Cook peas, celery and onion as directed on package for peas; drain. Stir in margarine and salt.

MENU

HAM LOAF SUPERB

HOT MUSTARD FRUIT

BAKED SWEET POTATOES

GREEN PEAS
WITH CELERY
AND ONION

LIME YOGURT DESSERT
(PAGE 62)

6 TO 8 SERVINGS

Hot Turkey Salad

2 cups cut-up cooked turkey or chicken	2 tablespoons lemon juice
2 cups plain croutons	1 tablespoon finely chopped onion
2 cups thinly sliced celery	½ teaspoon salt
1 cup mayonnaise or salad dressing	½ cup shredded Cheddar cheese (about 2 ounces)
½ cup toasted slivered almonds	

Mix all ingredients except 1 cup of the croutons and the cheese. Pour into ungreased 2-quart casserole or baking dish, 12x7½x2 inches. Sprinkle with remaining croutons and the cheese. Cook uncovered in 350° oven until hot, 30 to 35 minutes.

☐ **Microwave Directions:** Prepare in 2-quart microwaveproof casserole. Cover tightly and microwave on high (100%) 3 minutes; rotate casserole ½ turn. Microwave until hot, 5 to 7 minutes longer.

To toast almonds in microwave, place ½ cup slivered almonds and 1 tablespoon margarine or butter in 9-inch microwaveproof pie plate. Microwave on high (100%), stirring every minute, until brown, 4 to 5 minutes.

Ham and Broccoli Scallop

1 package (5.5 ounces) au gratin potato mix	1 package (10 ounces) frozen chopped broccoli, partially thawed and broken apart
1½ to 2 cups cubed fully cooked smoked ham	

Prepare potatoes as directed on package except—use 2-quart casserole and omit margarine. Stir in ham and broccoli. Cook uncovered 45 to 50 minutes.

Orange Sherbet Salad

1 cup boiling water	1 cup orange sherbet
1 package (3 ounces) orange-flavored gelatin	1 can (11 ounces) mandarin orange segments, drained

Pour boiling water on gelatin in bowl; stir until gelatin is dissolved. Add orange sherbet; stir until melted. Stir in orange segments. Pour into 4-cup mold; refrigerate until firm.

Casual Get-Togethers

Good feelings, good fellowship, togetherness—that's the spirit of the season. Entertain before or after the Christmas pageant with the Beef Burgundy menu. Entice helpers to trim the tree with zesty Ham and Cheese Bunwiches (easy to increase for a larger crowd). Warm up skaters with something hot and hearty—Minestrone, for example. Offer punch and a hearty snack to the neighborhood carolers. This is how traditions get started!

Ham and Cheese Bunwiches

1 loaf (1 pound) frozen rye or whole wheat bread dough
Vegetable oil
Margarine or butter
2 tablespoons mayonnaise or salad dressing
1 tablespoon prepared mustard
1 teaspoon prepared horseradish
6 slices fully cooked smoked ham
6 slices Swiss cheese

Thaw dough according to package directions. Divide into 6 equal pieces and shape each into flattened ball. Place in lightly greased baking pan, 13x9x2 inches. Let rise until double, about 1 hour. Brush lightly with oil.

Heat oven to 350°. Bake buns until golden brown, 20 to 25 minutes. Cool. Cut buns into halves; spread cut sides with margarine. Mix mayonnaise, mustard and horseradish; spread on half of each bun. Place 1 slice each ham and cheese in each bun. Assemble and wrap each bunwich in aluminum foil. Place foil-wrapped bunwiches on cookie sheet. Heat in 350° oven until hot, 20 to 25 minutes.

Cinnamon-Applesauce Salad

Heat ¼ to ½ cup red cinnamon candies and ½ cup water, stirring frequently, until candies are melted. Pour on 1 package (3 ounces) lemon-flavored gelatin in bowl; stir until gelatin is dissolved. Stir in 1½ cups applesauce. Pour into 3- or 4-cup mold or baking pan, 8x8x2 inches. Refrigerate until firm.

MENU

HAM AND CHEESE BUNWICHES
PICKLED BEETS
VEGETABLE RELISHES
CINNAMON-APPLESAUCE SALAD
HOLIDAY COOKIES

6 SERVINGS

Minestrone

2 pounds ground beef
1 large onion, chopped (about
    1 cup)
1 clove garlic, finely chopped
1 can (28 ounces) whole
    tomatoes
1 can (15 ounces) kidney beans
1 can (12 ounces)
    vacuum-packed whole
    kernel corn
2 stalks celery, sliced (about
    1 cup)
2 cups shredded cabbage
    (about ¼ head)
2 small zucchini, sliced
    (about 2 cups)
1 cup uncooked elbow
    macaroni or broken
    spaghetti
3 cups water
½ cup red wine or water
2 teaspoons instant beef
    bouillon
1½ teaspoons salt
1½ teaspoons Italian
    seasoning

Cook and stir ground beef, onion and garlic in Dutch oven until beef is light brown; drain. Stir in tomatoes (with liquid), kidney beans (with liquid) and remaining ingredients; break up tomatoes with fork.

Heat to boiling; reduce heat. Cover and simmer, stirring occasionally, until macaroni and vegetables are tender, about 10 minutes.

Do-Ahead Tip: After browning beef, stir in all ingredients except macaroni; cover and refrigerate no longer than 24 hours. About 20 minutes before serving, add macaroni. Heat to boiling; continue as directed above.

Parmesan Bread Sticks

Heat oven to 425°. Cut 1 loaf (1 pound) French bread into 5 pieces, each about 4 inches long; cut each piece lengthwise into 6 sticks. Brush cut sides with ¾ cup margarine or butter, melted; sprinkle with ¼ cup grated Parmesan cheese. Place sticks in ungreased jelly roll pan, 15½x10½x1 inch. Bake until golden, about 8 minutes. *30 bread sticks.*

Hot Cran-Apple Cider

2 quarts apple cider
1½ quarts cranberry juice
    cocktail
¼ cup packed brown sugar, if
    desired
4 three-inch sticks cinnamon
1½ teaspoons whole cloves
1 lemon, thinly sliced

Heat all ingredients to boiling in large kettle; reduce heat. Simmer uncovered until flavors are blended, about 15 minutes. Remove cinnamon, cloves and lemon slices. Float fresh lemon slices in each cup if desired. Allow about 1 cup for each serving.

Beef Burgundy

2½ pounds beef boneless chuck, tip or round (1 to 1¼ inches thick)
¼ cup vegetable oil
3 tablespoons flour
2 teaspoons salt
2 teaspoons instant beef bouillon
¼ teaspoon dried marjoram leaves
¼ teaspoon dried thyme leaves
⅛ teaspoon pepper
1¼ cups red Burgundy or other dry red wine
¾ cup water
5 medium onions, sliced, or 12 small whole onions
8 ounces mushrooms, cut into halves
Snipped parsley

Cut beef lengthwise into ¼-inch strips; cut strips into 2- to 3-inch pieces. (For easier cutting, partially freeze beef.) Cook and stir beef in oil in 4-quart Dutch oven over medium heat until brown; drain. Sprinkle beef with flour, salt, instant bouillon, marjoram, thyme and pepper. Stir in wine, water and onions. Heat to boiling; reduce heat. Cover and simmer until beef is tender, about 1 hour. Stir in mushrooms. Cover and simmer until mushrooms are done, 10 to 15 minutes. Sprinkle with parsley.

Mixed Green Salad with Parmesan Walnuts

1 small head lettuce
1 small bunch leaf lettuce
½ small bunch endive
4 ounces spinach
¼ cup oil and vinegar salad dressing
Parmesan Walnuts (below)

Tear greens into bite-size pieces (12 cups). Toss with salad dressing until greens are well coated. Toss with ½ to 1 cup Parmesan Walnuts.

PARMESAN WALNUTS

1 tablespoon margarine or butter
⅛ teaspoon hickory smoked salt
⅛ teaspoon salt
1 cup walnuts
2 tablespoons grated Parmesan cheese

Heat margarine, hickory salt and salt in baking pan, 9x9x2 inches, in 350° oven until margarine is bubbly, 2 to 3 minutes. Stir in walnuts; heat 5 minutes. Sprinkle with Parmesan cheese and toss until walnuts are evenly coated. Return to oven until cheese is lightly browned, 3 to 5 minutes. Cool. Refrigerate in airtight container no longer than 2 weeks. *1 cup walnuts.*

Sangría Punch

1⅓ cups lemon juice
⅔ cup orange juice
½ cup sugar

2 bottles (⅘ quart each) dry red wine

Strain juices; add sugar, stirring until dissolved. Just before serving, mix juice mixture and wine in pitcher. Add ice; serve in punch cups. Decorate cups with twists of lemon peel if desired. Allow about ½ cup for each serving.

Parmesan Bubble Loaf

1 package active dry yeast
¼ cup warm water (105 to 115°)
¾ cup lukewarm milk (scalded then cooled)
¼ cup sugar
1 teaspoon salt
1 egg
¼ cup margarine or butter

3½ to 3¾ cups all-purpose flour
½ cup margarine or butter, melted
1¼ cups grated Parmesan cheese (about 5 ounces)
Guacamole Dip (below)
Sliced fully cooked smoked ham

Dissolve yeast in warm water. Stir in milk, sugar, salt, egg, ¼ cup margarine and 2 cups of the flour. Beat until smooth. Mix in enough remaining flour to make dough easy to handle.

Turn dough onto lightly floured surface; knead until smooth and elastic, about 5 minutes. Place in greased bowl; turn greased side up. Cover; let rise in warm place until double, about 2 hours.

Line tube pan, 10x4 inches, with aluminum foil; grease. Punch down dough. Turn onto lightly floured surface; divide into 24 equal pieces. Dip each piece into melted margarine, roll in Parmesan cheese. Place 12 pieces in pan in one layer. Arrange second layer of 12 pieces on top of first. Cover; let rise until double.

Heat oven to 375°. Bake 35 minutes. Remove from pan. Serve warm with Guacamole Dip and thin slices of ham. Serve a mustard sauce as a dip for the ham if desired.

GUACAMOLE DIP

2 avocados, cut up
1 medium onion, finely chopped (about ½ cup)
1 or 2 green chilies, finely chopped
1 tablespoon lemon juice
1 teaspoon salt

½ teaspoon coarsely ground pepper
½ teaspoon ascorbic acid mixture
1 medium tomato, finely chopped (about ¾ cup)

Beat avocados, onion, chilies, lemon juice, salt, pepper and ascorbic acid mixture until creamy. Stir in tomato. Cover and refrigerate at least 1 hour. *About 2 cups dip.*

MENU

SANGRÍA PUNCH
PARMESAN BUBBLE LOAF
GUACAMOLE DIP
TORTILLA CHIPS
CHERRY TOMATOES   OLIVES
SALTED NUTS
HOLIDAY COOKIES

12 SERVINGS

Parmesan Bubble Loaf

Open Houses

"Come by any time between 5 and 7." It's a delightful way to entertain neighbors, friends and co-workers (the more mixed the group, the better). Set out an array of appetizers, a sweet or two and perhaps a punch, and you have the makings of an open house. Follow these menus, or mix and match. Just be sure to prepare ahead and enjoy along with your guests.

Opposite: A gala holiday spread. Clockwise from top: Wassail (page 152), Green Goddess Dip (this page), Teriyaki Chicken Wings (page 147), Party Deviled Eggs (page 146), Cherry Tomato Blossoms (page 147), Miniature Ham Puffs (page 146), Liver Pâté (this page) and Salmon Party Ball (page 146) in the center

Green Goddess Dip

¾ cup dairy sour cream
¾ cup mayonnaise or salad dressing
1 can (2 ounces) anchovy fillets, drained and finely chopped

⅓ cup snipped parsley
3 tablespoons snipped chives
1 tablespoon vinegar
1 clove garlic, crushed
¼ teaspoon salt
⅛ teaspoon pepper

Mix all ingredients. Cover and refrigerate at least 8 hours. Serve with assorted raw vegetable dippers.   *2 cups dip.*

Liver Pâté

1 package (8 ounces) frozen chicken livers, thawed
½ cup water
1 chicken bouillon cube or 1 teaspoon instant chicken bouillon
1 small onion, chopped (about ¼ cup)

¼ teaspoon dried thyme leaves
3 slices bacon, crisply fried and crumbled
¼ cup margarine or butter, softened
¼ teaspoon dry mustard
⅛ teaspoon garlic salt
Dash of pepper

Mix chicken livers, water, bouillon cube, onion and thyme in 1-quart saucepan. Heat to boiling; reduce heat. Simmer uncovered until livers are done, about 15 minutes. Cool mixture; drain and reserve ¼ cup broth.

Mix chicken livers, reserved broth and the remaining ingredients in small mixer bowl or blender container. Beat on low speed of mixer and then on high speed until creamy or beat in blender until smooth, about 30 seconds. Place in serving dish. Cover and refrigerate at least 3 hours. Garnish with parsley if desired.   *8 servings.*

Note: Pâté can be formed in individual servings, as pictured. After refrigerating, dip small ice-cream scoop into pâté and place each scoop on small lettuce leaf. Garnish each with pimiento.

Salmon Party Ball

1 package (8 ounces) cream
   cheese, softened
1 can (16 ounces) salmon,
   drained and flaked
1 tablespoon finely chopped
   onion

1 tablespoon lemon juice
¼ teaspoon liquid smoke
¼ teaspoon salt
⅓ cup chopped nuts
¼ cup snipped parsley

Mix all ingredients except nuts and parsley; shape mixture into a ball. Cover and refrigerate at least 8 hours but no longer than 4 days. Mix nuts and parsley; coat ball with mixture.　*1 salmon ball.*

Miniature Ham Puffs

1 cup water
½ cup margarine or butter
1 cup all-purpose flour
4 eggs
3 cans (4½ ounces each)
   deviled ham

1 tablespoon horseradish
¾ teaspoon pepper
¾ teaspoon onion salt
⅓ cup dairy sour cream

Heat oven to 400°. Heat water and margarine to rolling boil in 3-quart saucepan. Stir in flour. Stir vigorously over low heat until mixture forms a ball, about 1 minute; remove from heat. Beat in eggs, all at once, until smooth and glossy. Drop dough by slightly rounded teaspoonfuls onto ungreased cookie sheet. Bake until puffed, golden brown and dry, about 25 minutes. Cool on wire racks.

Blend deviled ham, horseradish, pepper, onion salt and sour cream; refrigerate. Just before serving, cut off tops of puffs with sharp knife; remove any filaments of soft dough. Fill each puff with rounded teaspoonful of ham mixture.　*5 to 6 dozen appetizers.*

Do-Ahead Tip: Puffs can be baked ahead and frozen no longer than 1 month. Thaw unwrapped at room temperature about 30 minutes. Fill as directed.

Party Deviled Eggs

12 hard-cooked eggs
1 teaspoon salt
1 teaspoon dry mustard

½ teaspoon pepper
⅓ cup mayonnaise or salad
   dressing

Cut peeled eggs lengthwise into halves. Slip out yolks; mash with fork. Mix in salt, mustard, pepper and mayonnaise. Fill whites with egg yolk mixture, heaping it lightly. Arrange eggs on large serving plate. Garnish each deviled egg half with cooked shrimp, rolled anchovy fillet or sliced pimiento-stuffed olive if desired. Cover and refrigerate no longer than 24 hours.　*2 dozen appetizers.*

Teriyaki Chicken Wings

3 to 3½ pounds chicken wings (about 20)	2 tablespoons sugar
½ cup catsup	1 teaspoon salt
¼ cup dry white wine	½ teaspoon ground ginger
¼ cup soy sauce	1 clove garlic, crushed

Cut each chicken wing at joints to make 3 pieces; discard tips. Place chicken in ungreased baking dish, 13x9x2 inches. Mix remaining ingredients; pour on chicken. Cover and refrigerate, turning chicken occasionally, at least 1 hour.

Heat oven to 375°. Drain chicken, reserving marinade. Place chicken on rack in aluminum foil-lined broiler pan. Bake 30 minutes. Brush with reserved marinade. Turn chicken; bake, brushing occasionally with marinade, until tender, 30 to 40 minutes. *8 to 12 servings.*

Cherry Tomato Blossoms

1 pint medium to large cherry tomatoes (about 24)	2 ounces cream cheese, cut into ½-inch cubes (about 24)

Place tomatoes stem side down; cut each almost through to bottom into fourths (larger tomatoes can be cut into sixths). Place cream cheese cube in center of each tomato. Top with small parsley sprigs if desired. *About 2 dozen appetizers.*

Olive-Cheese Balls

2 cups shredded sharp natural Cheddar cheese (about 8 ounces)	½ cup margarine or butter, melted
1¼ cups all-purpose flour	About 36 small pimiento-stuffed olives, drained

Mix cheese and flour; mix in margarine. (Work dough with hands if it seems dry.) Mold 1 teaspoon dough around each olive; shape into ball. Place 2 inches apart on ungreased cookie sheet. Cover and refrigerate at least 1 hour. Heat oven to 400°. Bake until set, 15 to 20 minutes. *3 to 4 dozen appetizers.*

Do-Ahead Tip: To freeze, place molded balls of dough on ungreased cookie sheet. Freeze until firm, at least 2 hours. Place cheese balls in plastic freezer bags. Seal, label and return to freezer. Freeze no longer than 3 months. About 25 minutes before serving, heat oven to 400°. Remove cheese balls from freezer; place 2 inches apart on ungreased cookie sheet. Bake until hot, about 20 minutes.

MENU

GUACAMOLE DIP (PAGE 143)

TORTILLA CHIPS

CRISP VEGETABLE RELISHES

OLIVE-CHEESE BALLS
OR
MEXICAN CHEESE PUFFS

CHICKEN BITES

NUTTY CEREAL SNACK

OLD-FASHIONED FRUITCAKE
(PAGE 54)

Mexican Cheese Puffs

1 cup buttermilk baking mix
3 tablespoons margarine or
    butter, softened
1 egg

3 tablespoons chopped green
    chilies
1 cup shredded Cheddar
    cheese (about 4 ounces)

Heat oven to 400°. Mix baking mix, margarine, egg and chilies; stir in cheese. Drop dough by rounded teaspoonfuls about 1 inch apart onto greased cookie sheet. Bake until golden brown, 10 to 12 minutes.   *About 2 dozen appetizers.*

Sausage Cheese Puffs: Substitute ¼ cup finely crumbled uncooked bulk pork sausage for the margarine. Bake 12 to 15 minutes.

Do-Ahead Tip: Dough can be placed in bowl or spooned onto cookie sheet, covered and refrigerated no longer than 24 hours.

Chicken Bites

4 chicken breasts, boned and
    skinned
1 cup finely crushed round
    buttery crackers (about 24)
½ cup grated Parmesan cheese
¼ cup finely chopped walnuts

1 teaspoon dried thyme leaves
1 teaspoon dried basil leaves
½ teaspoon seasoned salt
¼ teaspoon pepper
½ cup margarine or butter,
    melted

Cover 2 cookie sheets with aluminum foil. Cut chicken into 1-inch pieces. Mix cracker crumbs, Parmesan cheese, walnuts, thyme, basil, seasoned salt and pepper.

Heat oven to 400°. Dip chicken pieces into melted margarine, then into crumb mixture. Place chicken pieces about ½ inch apart on cookie sheets. Bake uncovered until golden brown, 20 to 25 minutes.   *About 6 dozen appetizers.*

Nutty Cereal Snack

4 cups crispy corn puff cereal
2 cups pretzel sticks
2 cups cashews, peanuts or
    mixed nuts
½ cup margarine or butter

1 teaspoon celery salt
1 teaspoon garlic salt
1 teaspoon Worcestershire
    sauce

Heat oven to 300°. Mix cereal, pretzels and cashews in ungreased baking pan, 13x9x2 inches. Heat margarine in 1-quart saucepan until melted; remove from heat. Stir in celery salt, garlic salt and Worcestershire sauce. Pour over cereal mixture, tossing until thoroughly coated. Bake uncovered, stirring occasionally, 25 minutes.   *About 8 cups snack.*

Deviled Ham Dip

¼ cup milk
1 package (8 ounces) cream cheese, softened
½ cup mayonnaise or salad dressing
1 tablespoon prepared mustard
¼ cup chopped green onions (with tops)

2 teaspoons prepared horseradish
⅛ teaspoon red pepper sauce
Dash of Worcestershire sauce
1 can (4½ ounces) deviled ham
Paprika

Stir milk, 1 tablespoon at a time, into cream cheese. Mix in mayonnaise, mustard, green onions, horseradish, pepper sauce and Worcestershire sauce. Stir in deviled ham; sprinkle with paprika. Cover and refrigerate at least 1 hour. *About 2½ cups dip.*

Spinach-Cheese Balls

1 package (10 ounces) frozen chopped spinach, thawed and drained
2 eggs, beaten
¾ cup seasoned dry bread crumbs
½ cup grated Parmesan cheese

⅓ cup margarine or butter, melted
1 small onion, finely chopped (about ¼ cup)
½ teaspoon poultry seasoning
¼ teaspoon garlic powder
⅛ teaspoon pepper

Press any remaining liquid from spinach. Mix spinach and remaining ingredients. Heat oven to 350°. Shape mixture into 1-inch balls; roll in additional Parmesan cheese if desired. Place on ungreased cookie sheet. Bake until light brown and firm, about 15 minutes. Serve hot. *About 3½ dozen appetizers.*

Do-Ahead Tip: Before baking, Spinach-Cheese Balls can be covered and refrigerated no longer than 24 hours. Or freeze in single layer until firm, about 1½ hours. Place in freezer containers and freeze no longer than 2 weeks. Bake at 350° 15 minutes.

Smoked Turkey Canapés

1 package (3 ounces) smoked sliced turkey, finely chopped
1 small stalk celery, finely chopped (about ¼ cup)
1 tablespoon finely chopped onion

⅓ cup mayonnaise or salad dressing
⅛ teaspoon liquid smoke
Crackers

Mix turkey, celery, onion, mayonnaise and liquid smoke. Cover and refrigerate at least 3 hours. Serve on crackers. *About 16 canapés.*

Party Punches

Spread joy with a toast round the punch bowl. Mix a sparkling fruit combo to serve before dinner . . . lift the spirits of a brunch punch with a decorative ice ring . . . offer Southern Custard Eggnog as dessert . . . serve Wassail or Glögg just because it wouldn't be Christmas without them.

Southern Custard Eggnog

Soft Custard (below)
1 cup chilled whipping cream
2 tablespoons powdered
   sugar
½ teaspoon vanilla
½ cup rum
1 or 2 drops yellow food color,
   if desired
Ground nutmeg

Prepare Soft Custard. Just before serving, beat whipping cream, powdered sugar and vanilla in chilled small mixer bowl until stiff. Stir rum and food color into chilled custard. Stir 1 cup of the whipped cream gently into custard.

Pour eggnog into small punch bowl. Drop remaining whipped cream in 4 or 5 mounds onto eggnog. Sprinkle nutmeg on whipped cream mounds. Serve immediately.   *10 servings (about ½ cup each).*

SOFT CUSTARD
3 eggs, slightly beaten
⅓ cup sugar
   Dash of salt
2½ cups milk
1 teaspoon vanilla

Mix eggs, sugar and salt in heavy 2-quart saucepan. Stir in milk gradually. Cook over low heat, stirring constantly, until mixture just coats a metal spoon, 15 to 20 minutes.

Remove custard from heat; stir in vanilla. Place saucepan in cold water until custard is cool. (If custard curdles, beat vigorously with hand beater until smooth.) Cover and refrigerate at least 2 hours but no longer than 24 hours.

Raspberry Shrub

Cook 4 packages (10 ounces each) frozen raspberries, thawed, 10 minutes. Rub through strainer with wooden spoon; cool. Add 1 can (6 ounces) frozen lemonade concentrate, thawed. Just before serving, stir in 2 quarts ginger ale, chilled.   *24 servings (about ½ cup each).*

Cranberry-Lemon Punch

3 quarts water
2 cups sugar
2 cups strong tea
2 cans (6 ounces each) frozen
    lemonade concentrate,
    thawed

2 quarts cranberry juice cocktail
1 quart apple juice
2 cups orange juice

Heat water and sugar to boiling, stirring constantly, until sugar is dissolved; cool. Prepare tea, using 1 tablespoon loose tea or 3 tea bags and 2 cups boiling water; cool. Refrigerate all ingredients. Just before serving, mix in large punch bowl. *60 servings (about ½ cup each).*

Rosé Punch

2 bottles (⅘ quart each) rosé,
    chilled
½ cup grenadine syrup, chilled
½ cup lemon juice, chilled

1 quart ginger ale, chilled
Della Robbia Ice Ring
    (below)

Mix rosé, grenadine syrup and lemon juice in large punch bowl. Stir in ginger ale. Float ice ring in bowl. *22 servings (about ½ cup each).*

Creamy Rosé Punch: Spoon 1 pint raspberry sherbet into bowl.

DELLA ROBBIA ICE RING
Fill a 6-cup ring mold about ¾ full of water. Freeze until solid, about 8 hours. Arrange assorted fruit and leaves on top, then pour in about ½ inch water; freeze. Unmold and float the ice ring fruit side up in punch bowl.

Sparkling Cranberry Punch

Mix 2 quarts cranberry juice cocktail, chilled, and 1 can (6 ounces) frozen lemonade concentrate, thawed, in large punch bowl. Just before serving, stir in 1 quart sparkling water, chilled. *25 servings (about ½ cup each).*

Frosty Lime Punch

2 cans (6 ounces each) frozen
    limeade concentrate,
    thawed
3 cups cold water

2 bottles (12 ounces each)
    lemon-lime carbonated
    beverage, chilled
1 cup lime sherbet

Mix limeade concentrate, cold water and carbonated beverage in large punch bowl. Spoon scoops of sherbet into bowl. Serve immediately. *15 servings (about ½ cup each).*

To make ice ring pictured below, arrange thin citrus slices and cranberries in 6-cup ring mold. Pour water into mold to partially cover fruit; freeze. When frozen, add water to fill mold ¾ full; freeze. Unmold and float fruit side up in punch bowl.

Cranberry-Lemon Punch

Wassail

1 gallon apple cider
2 teaspoons whole allspice
2 teaspoons whole cloves
2 three-inch sticks cinnamon

⅔ cup sugar
Oranges slices, studded
    with cloves

Heat cider, allspice, cloves, cinnamon and sugar to boiling; reduce heat. Cover and simmer 20 minutes. Strain punch and pour into heatproof punch bowl. Float orange slices in bowl.   *32 servings (about ½ cup each).*

Glögg

10 whole cloves
 7 cardamom pods, crushed
 2 sticks cinnamon
 1 piece gingerroot, about ½
     inch, if desired
 2 cups water
10 whole blanched almonds,
     cut lengthwise into halves

1¾ cups raisins
 1 cup pitted large prunes
 1 orange, cut into fourths
 2 bottles (⅘ quart each) dry
     red wine
1¾ cups brandy
1¾ cups vodka
 ⅓ cup sugar

Tie cloves, cardamom, cinnamon and gingerroot in cheesecloth bag. Heat spice bag, water, almonds, raisins, prunes and orange to boiling in Dutch oven; reduce heat. Cover and simmer 45 minutes. Remove spice bag, prunes and orange. (Reserve prunes for eating if desired.) Stir in remaining ingredients. Cover and heat until mixture begins to bubble. Ladle almond half and a few raisins into each cup before filling with hot Glögg.   *24 servings (½ cup each).*

Hot Cinnamon Cider

 3 quarts apple cider
 ⅓ cup red cinnamon candies

 1 tablespoon whole allspice
 3 tablespoons honey

Heat cider, cinnamon candies and allspice to boiling; reduce heat. Cover and simmer 5 minutes. Remove allspice; stir in honey.
24 servings (about ½ cup each).

Opposite: Christmas gifts from the kitchen. Left to right: Pineapple-Apricot Jam (page 155), Marzipan Cookies (page 166), Apricot-Cherry Cordial (page 162), Herbed Vinegar (page 160), Candied Citrus Peel (page 167) and Meringue Mushrooms (page 167) in the foreground

In the Spirit of Giving

Gifts of Food

When a gift comes from your own kitchen, the "especially for you" is special indeed. Exchange the hectic pace of department stores for the tantalizing aroma of fresh-baked breads. Avoid the problems of wrong sizes, wrong colors and duplicate gifts. Forget all about those last-minute forays and start stocking up a collection of homemade delectables at your own pace—to pick and choose from when Christmas arrives.

Here are our "recipes for the giving," truly food for thought—cookies and candies, jams and spreads, special dressings for salads, a seasoned salt, herbed vinegars, jumbo-size cookies and many more . . . plus a host of ideas for just-right wrappings. Here, too, are two handsome gingerbread constructions: an easy-to-make chalet and a gay Christmas sleigh, with its own team of reindeer—either would be perfect as a party-table centerpiece. With choices like these, it's easy to rediscover the special joys of making and giving in the true spirit of Christmas.

Apple-Pepper Jelly

2 cups water
1 can (6 ounces) frozen apple juice concentrate, thawed
1 package (1¾ ounces) powdered fruit pectin

3¾ cups sugar
1 to 2 tablespoons crushed red pepper
⅛ teaspoon red food color

Stir water, apple juice concentrate and pectin in 3-quart saucepan until pectin is dissolved. Heat to boiling, stirring constantly. Add sugar and red pepper; heat to rolling boil, stirring constantly. Remove from heat; strain. Stir in red food color. Immediately pour into hot sterilized jars or glasses or freezer containers. Cover tightly; cool. Refrigerate no longer than 4 weeks or freeze no longer than 2 months. Serve with meat.   *About 4 half-pints jelly.*

Grape Jelly: Substitute 1 can (6 ounces) frozen grape juice concentrate for the apple juice concentrate. Omit red pepper and food color.

Tangerine Jelly: Substitute 1 can (6 ounces) frozen tangerine juice concentrate for the apple juice concentrate. Omit red pepper and food color.

Lime Jelly

3 cups sugar
1 cup water
1 can (6 ounces) frozen limeade
  concentrate, thawed
2 tablespoons lemon juice

5 drops green food color
2 drops yellow food color
1 pouch (3 ounces) liquid fruit
  pectin

Heat sugar and water to boiling in Dutch oven, stirring occasionally. Boil and stir 1 minute; remove from heat. Stir in limeade concentrate, lemon juice and food colors. Stir in pectin. Skim off foam; immediately pour into hot sterilized jars or glasses or freezer containers. Cover tightly; cool. Refrigerate no longer than 4 weeks or freeze no longer than 2 months. *Four 7-ounce jars or six 5-ounce glasses.*

Strawberry-Orange Spread

2 packages (10 ounces each)
  frozen strawberries,
  thawed
1 package (1¾ ounces)
  powdered fruit pectin

1 tablespoon grated orange
  peel
½ cup orange juice
3½ cups sugar

Mix strawberries, pectin, orange peel and orange juice in 3-quart saucepan until pectin is dissolved. Heat over high heat, stirring constantly, to rolling boil, about 2 minutes. Add sugar. Heat to rolling boil, stirring constantly; remove from heat. Skim off foam. Immediately pour into hot sterilized jars or glasses or freezer containers. Cover tightly; cool. Refrigerate or freeze no longer than 3 months. *About 4 half-pints spread.*

Pineapple-Apricot Jam

1 can (20 ounces) crushed
  pineapple
1 jar (6 ounces) maraschino
  cherries, drained and cut
  up (reserve ⅓ cup syrup)
1 package (8 ounces) dried
  apricots, cut into fourths

¼ cup water
3½ cups sugar
2 tablespoons lemon juice
1 pouch (3 ounces) liquid
  fruit pectin

Heat pineapple (with syrup), reserved cherry syrup, the apricots and water to boiling in Dutch oven, stirring occasionally; reduce heat. Cover and simmer, stirring occasionally, until apricots are tender, about 10 minutes.

Stir in sugar, lemon juice and cherries. Heat to full rolling boil over high heat, stirring constantly. Boil and stir 1 minute. Remove from heat; stir in pectin. Pour into hot sterilized jars or glasses or freezer containers. Cover tightly; cool. Refrigerate or freeze no longer than 3 months. *About 5 half-pints jam.*

Strawberry-Orange Spread

Raspberry-Rhubarb Jam

8 cups cut-up fresh rhubarb or
   2 packages (16 ounces each)
   frozen rhubarb
6 cups sugar

2 packages (10 ounces each)
   frozen raspberries
2 packages (3 ounces each)
   raspberry-flavored gelatin

Mix rhubarb and sugar in Dutch oven. Let stand 30 minutes, stirring occasionally. Heat over medium heat, stirring occasionally, until sugar is dissolved. Heat to boiling; reduce heat. Simmer uncovered 15 minutes, stirring frequently. Add raspberries; heat to boiling. Remove from heat. Stir in gelatin until dissolved. Immediately pour into hot sterilized jars or glasses or freezer containers. Cover tightly; cool. Refrigerate or freeze no longer than 3 months. *About 8 half-pints jam.*

Strawberry-Rhubarb Jam: Substitute 2 packages (10 ounces each) frozen strawberries and 2 packages (3 ounces each) strawberry-flavored gelatin for the frozen raspberries and raspberry-flavored gelatin.

Cranberry Conserve

2 cups water
2 cups packed brown sugar
2 packages (12 ounces each)
   cranberries (6 cups)
2 tablespoons grated orange
   peel

4 oranges, peeled and chopped
2 apples, pared and chopped
1 cup chopped nuts

Mix water and brown sugar in Dutch oven. Heat to boiling; boil 1 minute. Stir in remaining ingredients except nuts. Heat to boiling; boil rapidly until cranberries pop and mixture thickens, about 20 minutes. Stir in nuts. Immediately pour into hot sterilized jars or glasses or freezer containers. Cover tightly; cool. Refrigerate or freeze no longer than 3 months. *About 5 half-pints conserve.*

Candied Pickle Sticks

1 quart whole sour or dill
   pickles, drained
3 cups sugar
¼ cup coarsely chopped
   pickled sweet cherry
   peppers

2 teaspoons instant minced
   onion
1 teaspoon celery seed
1 teaspoon mustard seed
½ teaspoon crushed dried hot
   peppers

Remove tips from pickles. Cut pickles into medium sticks; drain. Mix pickles and remaining ingredients in glass bowl. Cover and refrigerate at least 12 hours. Stir pickle mixture until all sugar is dissolved. Pack pickles in small jars. Add syrup to cover pickles. Cover and refrigerate at least 24 hours but no longer than 2 weeks. *1 quart pickle sticks.*

Keep an eye out for unusual containers, both pretty and practical, all year long. Look for the kind that can serve another purpose after the contents are gone.

Opposite: Sparkling treats from your kitchen: Pineapple-Apricot Jam (page 155), Raspberry-Rhubarb Jam (this page), Lime Jelly (page 155) and Apple-Pepper Jelly (page 154)

Carrot-Pepper Relish

3 pounds carrots, cut into
⅓-inch slices
2 green peppers, chopped
2 medium onions, sliced
1 can (10¾ ounces) condensed
tomato soup
⅔ cup sugar
⅔ cup vinegar
½ cup vegetable oil
1 teaspoon salt
1 teaspoon Worcestershire
sauce
½ teaspoon pepper
½ teaspoon dry mustard
½ teaspoon dried dill weed

Cook carrots in 1 inch salted water (½ teaspoon salt to 1 cup water) until crisp-tender, 8 to 10 minutes; drain. Add green peppers and onions. Heat remaining ingredients to boiling, stirring occasionally. Remove from heat; cool 5 minutes. Pour over vegetables. Refrigerate no longer than 3 weeks.   *10 cups relish.*

Gourmet Olives

2 jars (about 7 ounces each)
large green olives
2 cans (about 7 ounces each)
ripe olives
¾ cup vegetable oil
3 tablespoons vinegar
1 tablespoon lemon juice
3 cloves garlic, finely chopped
10 peppercorns, crushed

Drain olives; transfer to large jar. Mix remaining ingredients and pour over olives. Cover and refrigerate 10 to 12 hours; shake olives occasionally to coat evenly. (If transferring to gift jars, divide olives and liquid evenly.) Olives can be stored in refrigerator no longer than 2 weeks. Drain well before serving.   *About 3 cups olives.*

Seasoned Coating Mix

2 cups fine dry bread crumbs
2 teaspoons paprika
1½ teaspoons salt
1½ teaspoons poultry
seasoning
1 teaspoon onion salt
1 teaspoon garlic salt
½ teaspoon pepper

Mix all ingredients. Store in tightly covered container.   *Enough for four 2½- to 3-pound broiler-fryer chickens (½ cup for each chicken) or 6 pounds fish (⅓ cup for each pound).*

To prepare 1 chicken, pour 2 tablespoons vegetable oil into jelly roll pan, 15½x10½x1 inch. Shake chicken, 2 or 3 pieces at a time, with ½ cup coating mix in plastic or paper bag until coated. Place skin side down in pan and cook uncovered in 375° oven until done, 45 to 60 minutes.

To prepare 1 pound fish, pour 1 tablespoon vegetable oil into baking pan, 12x7½x2 inches. Coat fish with ⅓ cup coating mix. Cook uncovered in 350° oven until fish flakes easily with fork, about 30 minutes.

Carrot-Pepper Relish

Party Cheese Balls

2 packages (8 ounces each)
    cream cheese, softened
1 package (4 ounces) blue
    cheese, crumbled (1 cup)
1 cup shredded sharp Cheddar
    cheese (about 4 ounces)

1 tablespoon brandy or
    Worcestershire sauce
1 teaspoon instant minced
    onion
  Snipped parsley or finely
    chopped nuts

A refrigerated gift may be ideal for a nearby neighbor. Remember to indicate the maximum storage time.

Mix all ingredients except parsley. Cover and refrigerate at least 3 hours. Shape mixture into 2 balls. Roll in parsley or chopped nuts. To store, wrap in plastic wrap and refrigerate no longer than 2 weeks. Cheese ball coated with chopped nuts can be wrapped and frozen no longer than 4 weeks. Thaw wrapped cheese ball in refrigerator about 24 hours before serving.   *Two 4-inch cheese balls.*

Liptauer Cheese Spread

1 package (8 ounces) cream
    cheese, softened
½ cup margarine or butter,
    softened
½ cup dairy sour cream

2 tablespoons anchovy paste
2 tablespoons snipped chives
1 tablespoon paprika
2 teaspoons capers
½ teaspoon dry mustard

Place all ingredients in blender container. Cover and blend on high speed, stopping blender occasionally to scrape sides, until smooth, about 1 minute. Spoon mixture into crocks or serving containers. Cover tightly and refrigerate until well chilled, 4 to 5 hours. Spread can be stored in refrigerator no longer than 2 weeks.   *2 cups spread.*

Toasted Sesame Butter

1 cup margarine or butter,
    softened
1 tablespoon Worcestershire
    sauce

2 teaspoons garlic salt
¼ cup toasted sesame seed

Beat margarine, Worcestershire sauce and garlic salt until completely mixed. Stir in toasted sesame seed. Refrigerate in tightly covered container no longer than 2 weeks. Serve as a topping for broiled steaks and hamburgers.   *1½ cups butter.*

Mustard Butter

1 cup margarine or butter,
    softened
¼ cup snipped parsley

½ cup prepared mustard
1 teaspoon onion salt

Mix all ingredients. Refrigerate in tightly covered container no longer than 2 weeks. Serve as a topping for broiled steaks and hamburgers.   *1½ cups butter.*

Lemon-Garlic Oil and Herbed
Vinegars

Seasoned Salt

1 cup salt	1 teaspoon celery seed
1 tablespoon paprika	½ teaspoon garlic powder
1 teaspoon black pepper	½ teaspoon dried marjoram
1 teaspoon dried chives	leaves
1 teaspoon dried parsley flakes	⅛ teaspoon ground red pepper

Place all ingredients in blender container. Cover and blend on high speed until herbs and seeds are finely chopped, about 30 seconds. Store in salt shakers or in tightly covered jar. Use as an all-purpose seasoning.   *About 1 cup salt.*

Herbed Vinegars

Cut sprigs of fresh dill, basil, tarragon or mint to fit height of bottle. Place herb in bottle, using handle of wooden spoon to push through neck of bottle if necessary. Fill bottle with white, cider or wine vinegar. Cap; let stand at room temperature at least 5 days to blend flavors.

Chive Vinegar: Place ¼ cup snipped chives in bottle. Fill with vinegar. Cap and let stand as directed above. Strain before using.

Garlic-Parsley Vinegar: Place 2 cloves garlic, peeled and speared on wooden skewer, and 3 sprigs fresh parsley in bottle. Fill with vinegar. Cap and let stand as directed above.

Strawberry Vinegar

Press 1 package (10 ounces) frozen strawberries, thawed, through strainer to measure ¾ cup. Heat strawberry juice, 3 cups white or cider vinegar and 1 cup sugar to boiling, stirring frequently. Boil and stir 1 minute. Cool. Pour into bottles; cover tightly. Use in salad dressings and marinades.   *1 quart vinegar.*

Raspberry Vinegar: Substitute 1 package (10 ounces) frozen raspberries, thawed, for the strawberries.

Lemon-Garlic Oil

Place 2 cloves garlic and 1 long spiral lemon peel, about ½ inch wide, in bottle. Add 1 to 1½ cups olive or vegetable oil. Cover and refrigerate at least 1 week to blend flavors. Refrigerate no longer than 2 months. Bring to room temperature before using. Use in salad dressings or to brush over fish or poultry before broiling. *1 to 1½ cups oil.*

Blue Cheese Dressing

2 cups salad dressing or
   mayonnaise
1 cup dairy sour cream
1 cup chili sauce
2 tablespoons sugar

2 teaspoons Worcestershire
   sauce
½ teaspoon garlic salt
4 ounces blue cheese,
   crumbled (1 cup)

Mix salad dressing, sour cream, chili sauce, sugar, Worcestershire sauce and garlic salt until smooth. Stir in blue cheese. Add small amount water or milk, if necessary, for desired consistency. Refrigerate in tightly covered container no longer than 3 weeks. *About 4½ cups dressing.*

Poppy Seed Dressing

1 cup vegetable oil
⅔ cup sugar
¼ cup vinegar
¼ cup lemon juice

1 to 2 teaspoons poppy seed
1 teaspoon salt
1 small onion, cut into fourths

Place all ingredients in blender container. Cover and blend on high speed until completely mixed. Refrigerate in tightly covered container no longer than 4 weeks. Serve on fruit or tossed salads. *2 cups dressing.*

Sweet-and-Sour Salad Dressing

1 cup vegetable oil
½ cup sugar
½ cup vinegar
1 tablespoon dried parsley
   flakes

2 teaspoons salt
⅛ teaspoon pepper
4 drops red pepper sauce

Shake all ingredients in tightly covered jar. Refrigerate no longer than 4 weeks. Serve on fruit or tossed salads.   *1½ cups dressing.*

Ruby French Dressing

1 cup vegetable oil
⅔ cup catsup
½ cup sugar
½ cup vinegar
2 tablespoons finely chopped
   onion

1 tablespoon lemon juice
1 teaspoon salt
1 teaspoon pepper
1 teaspoon dry mustard
1 teaspoon paprika

Shake all ingredients in tightly covered jar. Refrigerate no longer than 4 weeks. Shake well before using. Serve on fruit or tossed salads.   *2⅔ cups dressing.*

Spiced Orange Tea Mix

1 cup powdered orange
    breakfast drink mix
⅔ cup instant tea
⅓ cup presweetened lemonade
    mix

¼ cup sugar
½ teaspoon ground cinnamon
½ teaspoon ground cloves

Mix all ingredients. Store in tightly covered container. For each serving, place 2 to 3 teaspoons mix in cup. Fill with boiling apple cider, apple juice, cranberry juice or water; stir. For 6 servings (about ⅔ cup each), place ¼ to ⅓ cup mix in heatproof container; add 4 cups boiling liquid. *About 1⅔ cups mix.*

Spicy Mocha Mix

½ cup sugar
¼ cup freeze-dried coffee
¼ cup cocoa

1 teaspoon ground nutmeg
½ teaspoon ground cinnamon

Place all ingredients in blender container. Cover and blend on high speed 15 seconds; stir. Cover and blend until completely mixed, about 15 seconds. Store in tightly covered container.

For each serving, place 2 to 3 teaspoons mix in cup. Fill with boiling water; stir. Top with whipped topping if desired. For 6 servings (about ⅔ cup each), place ¼ to ⅓ cup mix in heatproof container; add 4 cups boiling water. *About 1 cup mix.*

Mocha Mix: Decrease cocoa to 2 tablespoons and omit spices.

Apricot-Cherry Cordial

1 package (8 ounces) dried
    apricots, each cut into
    fourths
1 package (8 ounces) dried
    pears or peaches, cut up
1 jar (10 ounces) maraschino
    cherries, drained and cut
    into halves

1½ cups sugar
1½ cups brandy
1½ cups vodka

Mix all ingredients in 2-quart jar. Cover tightly and let stand at room temperature 2 weeks, stirring mixture or inverting jar every day. Drain well, reserving fruit. Pour cordial into bottles and seal. *2½ cups cordial.*

Note: For a topping for ice cream or cake, mix reserved fruit, ½ cup coconut, ½ cup slivered almonds and ½ cup maple syrup or honey. Cover and refrigerate no longer than 1 week.

Cranberry Cordial

2 packages (12 ounces each)
   frozen cranberries,
   chopped

4 cups sugar
3 cups vodka

Mix all ingredients in 2-quart jar or crock. Cover tightly and let stand at room temperature 2 weeks, stirring mixture or inverting jar every day. Strain; pour cordial into bottles and seal. Serve well chilled or over cracked ice.   *5 cups cordial.*

Note: After straining cordial, cranberries can be used with water to make an ice ring for a holiday punch.

Coffee Liqueur

3 cups vodka
2 cups water
2 cups granulated sugar
2 cups packed brown sugar

⅔ cup freeze-dried coffee
1 vanilla bean or 1 teaspoon
   vanilla

Mix all ingredients in 2-quart jar. Cover tightly and let stand at room temperature 2 weeks. Pour liqueur into bottles and seal.
About 7½ cups liqueur.

Hot Fudge Sauce

1 can (13 ounces) evaporated
   milk
1 package (12 ounces) semisweet chocolate chips

1 cup sugar
1 tablespoon margarine or
   butter
1 teaspoon vanilla

Heat evaporated milk, chocolate chips and sugar over medium heat, stirring constantly, until chocolate is melted and mixture boils. Remove from heat; stir in margarine and vanilla. Pour into jars; cover tightly. Refrigerate no longer than 4 weeks. Serve warm over vanilla ice cream.   *3 cups sauce.*

Brandied Butterscotch Sauce

3 cups packed brown sugar
1 cup light corn syrup
½ cup margarine or butter

½ cup whipping cream
1 tablespoon brandy or 1
   teaspoon brandy flavoring

Heat brown sugar, corn syrup and margarine to boiling over medium heat, stirring constantly. Remove from heat; stir in whipping cream and brandy. Cool. Pour into jars; cover tightly. Refrigerate no longer than 3 months. Serve warm over vanilla ice cream.
3½ cups sauce.

Cranberry Cordial (this page) and
Apricot-Cherry Cordial (page 162)

Spicy Sugared Nuts

⅔ cup sugar
 1 teaspoon ground cinnamon
 ¼ teaspoon ground allspice

 ¼ teaspoon salt
 1 cup pecan halves
 1 cup whole almonds

Mix all ingredients in 8-inch skillet over low heat, stirring constantly, until sugar is melted and nuts are coated, about 20 minutes. Remove nuts from pan and cool on waxed paper; break apart. Store at room temperature.   *3 cups snack.*

Jumbo Holiday Cookies

Prepare dough as directed for Deluxe Sugar Cookies (page 6), Merry Christmas Molasses Cookies (page 7), Light Ginger Cookies (page 10), or Christmas Pinwheels (page 10). Cover and refrigerate dough as directed.

Roll dough ³⁄₁₆ inch thick on lightly floured cloth-covered board. Cut into desired shapes with jumbo cookie cutters or cut around patterns traced from magazines, Christmas cards or storybook illustrations. Or for a personal touch, use one of your child's drawings as a pattern. (To enlarge patterns, see directions below.)

Bake cookies until light brown, 7 to 10 minutes. (For Merry Christmas Molasses Cookies, bake until no indentation remains.) Cool cookies 1 to 2 minutes; remove to wire rack. Glaze cookies with Thin Cookie Glaze (below) if desired.

THIN COOKIE GLAZE

2 cups powdered sugar
 2 tablespoons milk
 ¼ teaspoon almond extract

Red or green food color
 About ⅓ cup powdered sugar

Mix 2 cups powdered sugar, the milk and almond extract. Tint half of the mixture with 4 or 5 drops food color. Add additional milk, a few drops at a time, if necessary for glaze consistency. Place baked cookies on wire rack. Glaze cookies by pouring small amount of glaze over each cookie; spread to edge with spatula. Add enough powdered sugar to remaining glaze to make a frosting that can be used in a decorators' tube or envelope cone (page 7) and will hold its shape. Place in decorators' tube with #2 writing tip. Decorate glazed cookies as desired.   *Enough to glaze and decorate 8 to 10 jumbo cookies.*

To Enlarge a Pattern: First make a same-size tracing and draw a same-size grid right over it. Then make another grid of the desired size and draw in the pattern, square by square, exactly as it appears on the smaller grid. For example, if the same-size grid is made up of ½-inch squares and you want to double the size of the pattern, simply use an enlarged grid of 1-inch squares. Cut out the enlarged design and use it as your pattern.

Opposite: Jumbo Holiday Cookies

Marzipan Cookies

Marzipan Cookies

1 cup margarine or butter, softened	½ to 1 teaspoon almond extract
½ cup sugar	Food color
2½ cups all-purpose flour	

Mix margarine and sugar. Stir in flour and almond extract until mixture resembles coarse crumbs. Divide into 3 equal parts. Tint and shape dough as directed below. Place cookies on ungreased cookie sheet. Cover and refrigerate at least 30 minutes. Heat oven to 300°. Bake until set but not brown, about 30 minutes.
About 4 dozen.

APPLES

Mix red or green food color into part of dough. Shape into small balls. Insert small piece of stick cinnamon in top of each for stem end and whole clove in bottom of each for blossom end. Dilute red or green food color with water and brush over apples.

APRICOTS

Mix red and yellow food colors into part of dough. Shape into small balls. Make crease down 1 side of each with wooden pick. Insert whole clove in each for stem end. Dilute red food color with water and brush over apricots.

BANANAS

Mix yellow food color into part of dough. Shape into 3-inch rolls, tapering ends to resemble bananas. Slightly flatten sides of each to show planes of banana; curve each slightly. Paint on characteristic markings with mixture of red, yellow and blue food colors diluted with water.

ORANGES

Mix red and yellow food colors into part of dough. Shape into small balls. Insert whole clove in each for blossom end. Prick balls with blunt end of wooden pick to resemble texture of orange peel.

PEARS

Mix yellow food color into part of dough. Shape into small balls, then into cone shapes, rounding narrow end of each. Insert small piece of stick cinnamon in narrow end for stem. Dilute red food color with water and brush on "cheeks" of pears.

STRAWBERRIES

Mix red food color into part of dough. Shape into small balls, then into heart shapes (about ¾ inch high). Prick with blunt end of wooden pick for texture. Roll each in red sugar. Insert small piece of green-colored wooden pick or green dough into top of each for stem.

Note: Use liquid food color for light colors, paste food color for deeper colors. Paste food color is available through mail-order baking equipment stores.

Meringue Mushrooms

2 egg whites	Cocoa
¼ teaspoon cream of tartar	Chocolate Decorators'
½ cup sugar	Frosting (below)

Cover 2 cookie sheets with heavy brown paper. Beat egg whites and cream of tartar in small mixer bowl until foamy. Beat in sugar, 1 tablespoon at a time; continue beating until stiff and glossy, about 5 minutes. Do not underbeat.

Heat oven to 200°. Fit decorators' tube with plain tip with ¼-inch opening (#10 or 11). Fill tube with meringue and fold top of bag. Hold tube upright and pipe out about 55 mushroom caps, each 1 to 1¼ inches in diameter. Sift cocoa over caps. Bake until firm, 45 to 50 minutes. Remove from oven; immediately turn caps upside down and make an indentation in bottom of each cap. Brush off excess cocoa with soft-bristled brush.

Pipe out about fifty-five ¾-inch upright cones on second cookie sheet for stems. Stems should have peaks which fit into mushroom caps. Bake until firm, 40 to 45 minutes. Remove from oven; cool. Prepare Chocolate Decorators' Frosting. To assemble mushrooms, spread small amount of frosting in indentation of each mushroom cap; insert stem and place upside down to dry. Store Meringue Mushrooms uncovered at room temperature. *About 55 candies.*

CHOCOLATE DECORATORS' FROSTING
Heat 1 square (1 ounce) unsweetened chocolate and 1 teaspoon margarine or butter until melted; remove from heat. Beat in 1 cup powdered sugar and 1 tablespoon hot water until smooth and of spreading consistency. If necessary, stir in additional hot water, 1 teaspoon at a time.

Candied Citrus Peel

3 oranges	¾ cup water
3 lemons	½ cup sugar
1½ cups sugar	

Cut peel of each orange and lemon into 4 sections with sharp knife. Remove peel carefully with fingers. Scrape white membrane from peel with spoon (back of peel will appear porous when membrane is removed). Cut peel lengthwise into strips ¼ inch wide. Heat peel and enough water to cover to boiling in 1½-quart saucepan; reduce heat. Simmer uncovered 30 minutes; drain. Repeat simmering process.

Heat 1½ cups sugar and ¾ cup water to boiling in 1½-quart saucepan, stirring constantly, until sugar is dissolved. Add peel. Simmer uncovered, stirring occasionally, 45 minutes. Drain in strainer. Roll peel in ½ cup sugar; spread on waxed paper to dry. Store in airtight container. *About 3 cups or 11 ounces candy.*

Meringue Mushrooms

What to Give?

Almost any gift from the kitchen gets an especially warm welcome. This chapter offers more than a score of good-to-give recipes, but you'll find many other candidates throughout the book. Following are just a few suggestions . . .

Breads
Yeast or quick, sweet or not, in a loaf or as rolls, any home-baked bread strikes a Christmas chord. Don't miss these:

Candy Cane Coffee Cakes (p. 74)
Carrot-Raisin Bread (p. 93)
Cloverleaf Rolls (p. 88)
Cranberry Coffee Cake (p. 82)
Fruited Christmas Wreath (p. 76)
Gumdrop Bread (p. 92)
Holiday Braid (p. 80)
Holiday Nut Bread (p. 92)
Lucia Buns (p. 75)
Poppy Seed Bread (p. 91)
Pumpkin-Date Bread (p. 91)

Cookies and Candies
It wouldn't be Christmas without traditional favorites, and every family seems to have its own treasured recipes. This year, add to your collection with these:

Almond Cookie Wreaths (p. 14)
Candied Fruit Cookies (p. 18)
Christmas Bells (p. 19)
Christmas Cookie Slices (p. 21)
Christmas Pinwheels (p. 10)
Cinnamon Stars (p. 11)
Krumkake (p. 35)
Magic Window Cookies (p. 12)
Mincemeat Bars (p. 24)
Paintbrush Cookies (p. 12)
Peppermint Candy Canes (p. 14)
Peppermint Pinwheels (p. 21)
Ribbon Bar Cookies (p. 21)
Rosettes (p. 35)
Santa Claus Cookies (p. 17)
Snowflake Cookies (p. 10)
Stained Glass Cookies (p. 6)
Sugarplum Cookies (p. 16)
Turtle Cookies (p. 16)
Brandied Stuffed Dates (p. 40)
Fudge Meltaways (p. 40)
No-Cook Divinity (p. 38)
Oven Caramel Corn (p. 43)
Peanut Butter Bonbons (p. 40)

Cookies That Travel Well
Share the bounty of your holiday baking with faraway friends and family. Choose a variety of cookies, pack carefully and send them off (for more about packing and mailing cookies, see page 171). Almost any bar cookie, provided it's not frosted, can be considered a good traveler. Here are some others:

Berlinerkranzer (p. 15)
Christmas Jewels (p. 22)
Coconut-Pecan Balls (p. 18)
Cranberry Cookies (p. 23)
Gumdrop Cookies (p. 22)
Lebkuchen (p. 11)
Light Ginger Cookies (p. 10)
Peppernuts (p. 14)
Sparkle Cookies (p. 32)
Spritz (p. 34)

Something Different
Let logic be your guide. Give a cheese spread to the bachelor next door, fix and freeze a soup or casserole for a working couple (be sure to include reheating instructions), present a decorated cake to a busy hostess (to protect the frosting, insert wooden picks at intervals into top and side, then cover with plastic wrap). Think about dips and hors d'oeuvres, doughnuts and popcorn balls, pies and cakes, sauces and syrups and seasoned butters. Consider these:

Beef-Taco Casserole (p. 134)
Chess Pie (p. 67)
Christmas Doughnuts (p. 86)
Della Robbia Apple Pie (p. 69)
Deviled Ham Dip (p. 149)
Drum Cake (p. 50)
Eggnog Cake (p. 47)
Hard Sauce (p. 57)
Liver Pâté (p. 144)
Minestrone (p. 140)
Olive-Cheese Balls (p. 147)
Raisin Sauce (p. 119)

Wrappings

Cans and bottles, jars and boxes — don't toss them away. Build up a collection, and transform them into personalized packagings for your special food gifts.

For Cans

Cans with plastic lids will serve the purpose best, and you'll find that recycling them is a relatively easy undertaking. Here are a few ideas:

• Cut giftwrap paper or fabric to fit, then paste to the can with white glue or fabric adhesive. (No pasting needed with adhesive-backed coverings.) Cover the lid to match if you like, or attach a pretty bow or a festive holiday decoration.

• Spray with paint and individualize with accents of ribbon or yarn, with stickers or with paper or fabric cutouts. Cover the lid with paper or felt, or spray with paint to match.

• Coat the can with white glue or rubber cement and coil yarn, a colorful cord or leftover upholstery welting around the side. Keep the rows close together, and remember to leave space at the top for the lid.

• Tuck tissue paper into the can before filling, or cover your food gift with plastic wrap.

For Jars and Bottles

Many food gifts are perfect for jars: candies, jams, relishes, mixes and so on. Since part of the pleasure is in the seeing, don't cover the jar. Use an attractive label to note the contents and concentrate on camouflaging the lid or cap.

• Make a fancy top by cutting a circle from scrap fabric (pinked edges are nice) and simply tying it around the lid or cap with ribbon or yarn.

• Use acrylic paint for a good finish and stick on a bow or other decoration. Glue ribbon around the edge of a wide lid.

• Or paint just the side of the lid and paste fabric or paper on top.

• Spread a thin coating of white glue over the side and top of the lid and, starting at the base, wind a colorful cord around the side and onto the top. When you reach the center, cut the cord, add glue to the end and tuck in. Or make the coil on the top and glue a ribbon around the edge.

For Plates and Trays

Colorful paper plates can be readily purchased, but trays are hard to come by. Make your own with cardboard and cover with giftwrap paper or foil.

• Cover the plate or tray of food with plastic wrap, securing the ends with tape on the underside; top with a holiday decoration. Or gather the ends of the wrap above the food and tie with ribbon or yarn.

For Boxes and Bags

You can give old boxes a new look by covering them — just make sure they're sturdy. And you'll find that bags are ideal for holding odd-shaped items.

• Cut giftwrap paper to fit the bottom and sides of box and glue in place; do the same with the lid. Tie with a ribbon.

• Cut a design in the lid of a box, then wrap with paper, trimming flush with the cutout. Overwrap with plastic wrap and your gift will show through.

• Make your own colorful bags by wrapping a box of facial tissues with foil or giftwrap paper, leaving one end open. Slip out the box, and you've made a bag.

• Cut out a design on one side of a bag and back the cutout with plastic wrap.

Double-Good Gifts

Why not combine your food gift with another gift? It doesn't have to be costly — just thoughtful. And who wouldn't appreciate an extra tray or serving plate, mixing bowl or freezer container.

● Offer cookies in a cookie jar, arranged on a new cookie sheet or in a canister.

● Include a package of wooden skewers with a jar of olives or pickles.

● Place candies in a brandy snifter or apothecary jar, or tuck them into an ice cube tray or a desk organizer.

● Set a steamed pudding in a brand-new mold.

● Pour seasoned oils, vinegars or salad dressing into cruets or one-of-a-kind bottles. Tie salad servers to the neck of the gift bottle.

● Give seasoned salt in its own shaker.

● Nest a spicy coffee mixture in a cheerful mug.

● Gather the ingredients for a special casserole and arrange them in a just-the-right-size baking dish. (Remember to include the recipe, too.) Add oven mitts or a pot holder.

● Think about using a pâté mold, ramekin or crock to go with a cheese spread. Tie a spreader to the bow.

● For the junior set, present popcorn balls or cookies in a toy boat or truck, lunch box or bicycle basket.

● Place a loaf of bread on a breadboard or cutting board.

● Set muffins in a basket lined with a holiday kitchen towel.

● Pile doughnuts in a punch bowl, colander or bread box.

Start Baking Early

"Next year I'm going to start in plenty of time." Sound familiar? Well, let this be the year to do it. Thanks to your freezer, you can prepare many of your holiday favorites well in advance and still preserve their fresh-baked quality. All it takes is a little know-how.

Guidelines for Freezing
● Make sure the temperature of your freezer is 0° or lower.
● Wrap food in moistureproof, vaporproof materials for maximum retention of flavor, moisture and nutrients. Before sealing, remove as much air from the package as possible.
● Label and date all packages.
● Don't turn your freezer into a Christmas catchall. You'll want to leave enough room for your everyday freezing needs. Here are some start-ahead spans:
Breads (baked) — 2 to 3 mos.
Cakes (unfrosted) — 3 to 4 mos.
   (frosted) — 2 to 3 mos.
Cookies (baked) — 3 to 4 mos.
Fruitcakes (baked) — 3 to 4 mos.
Pies (baked) — 1 to 2 mos.
   (unbaked) — 3 to 4 mos.
Steamed Puddings — 3 to 4 mos.

Special Tips for Breads
● Before freezing, cool completely and wrap tightly in moistureproof, vaporproof paper. Freezer bags will do the job too.
● Breads decorated with frostings and glazes can be frozen, but for the most attractive appearance, it's best to decorate just before giving.
● Keep breads wrapped while thawing at room temperature.

Special Tips for Cookies
● Freeze frosted cookies uncovered until they are firm, then pack in a single layer in an airtight container lined with plastic wrap or aluminum foil. Seal the lining, close container, label and freeze.
● Cool unfrosted cookies thoroughly. Pack in layers in freezer container, separating layers with plastic wrap or foil. Then seal the lining, close container, label and freeze.
● Rolls of refrigerator cookie dough can be wrapped and frozen no longer than 6 months. When ready to bake, slice the frozen dough with a sharp knife.

Mail Early Too
There's no such thing as "too early" when it comes to mailing Christmas cookies. Label your package "Open Before Christmas" and think how much more the recipient will enjoy your thoughtfulness during the holidays. If you mail before the Christmas rush, your package will reach its destination faster too. Check the post office for delivery time estimates of the various mail classifications. Here are some pointers:
● Choose plain or lightly glazed bar cookies or any of those in the Cookies That Travel Well list on page 168.

● Cut rolled cookies with rounded (not pointed) cutters to avoid crumbling and breakage.
● Wrap cookies in pairs, back to back, and place them in a can, box or other sturdy container.
● Fill each container as full as practical, padding the top with crushed paper to prevent shaking and breakage.
● Pack containers in a foil-lined corrugated or fiberboard packing box. For filler, use crumpled newspapers, shredded paper or shredded polyethylene foam. Don't use popcorn or cereal products as filler. They can absorb noxious fumes from airplane engines and become unsafe to eat.
● Seal packing box with "strapping tape"; wrap tightly in heavy paper and seal with tape.
● Write address on the package or gummed label in large, legible print. Cover address with transparent tape to protect it.

Cookie Chalet

Equipment

Grid paper for enlarging patterns
Heavy paper for patterns
1 or 2 cookie sheets (15½x12 inches)
Stockinet-covered rolling pin
Small sharp knife and scissors
Waxed paper
Small spatula
Decorators' tube or envelope cone
#3 and #10 tips for decorators' tube
Tray (base for chalet)

Preparation

1. Prepare Merry Christmas Molasses Cookie dough (page 7) as directed except—use light molasses, omit cinnamon and decrease baking soda to 1 teaspoon. Refrigerate at least 1 hour. Enlarge patterns according to scale (see Pattern Plan, page 174) and cut from heavy paper.

2. Roll 2 cups dough into rectangle, 15x10 inches, on lightly greased cookie sheet with floured stockinet-covered rolling pin. (If cookie sheet slips while rolling, place dampened towel underneath.) Heat oven to 375°. Place patterns on rectangle as shown in Diagram A. (The dough will expand during baking, so be sure to place the patterns at least ½ inch apart.) Cut around patterns with sharp knife; remove and reserve excess dough. Make slight marks with knife to indicate position of doors and windows. Bake until no indentation remains when touched, 5 to 6 minutes for small pieces, about 10 minutes for large pieces. Cool large pieces 1 to 2 minutes; remove to wire rack.

3. Repeat Step 2 except place patterns on rectangle as shown in Diagram B. Before baking, cut ⅜-inch-wide slot 1½ inches down from top of half of the trees; cut ⅜-inch-wide slot 1¾ inches up from bottom of remaining trees. After baking, while cookie trees are warm, insert bottom slot of one tree into top slot of another; repeat.

4. Roll about ½ cup dough ¹⁄₁₆ inch thick into rectangle, about 8x6 inches, on lightly greased cookie sheet. Cut into 2 rectangles, each 7x2¼ inches, for the shutters as shown in Diagram C; reserve excess dough. Cut each rectangle into seven 1-inch strips. Remove every other strip, leaving 8 shutters. Bake shutters 5 to 6 minutes.

5. Press remaining dough and the reserved dough into a ball (about 2 cups); knead in ⅓ cup cocoa. Roll 1½ cups cocoa dough into rectangle, 15x8 inches, on lightly greased cookie sheet. Cut 2 roof pieces as shown in Diagram D. Remove and reserve excess dough. Bake roof pieces about 10 minutes. Cool 1 to 2 minutes.

6. Roll all remaining dough ¹⁄₁₆ inch thick into square, about 9x9 inches, on lightly greased cookie sheet. Cut into 20 strips, each 9x⅜ inch, for trim. Remove every other strip, leaving 10 trim strips on cookie sheet. Bake trim strips 6 to 8 minutes.

7. Roll remaining dough about ⅛ inch thick; cut to form stones for path. Cut additional trees if desired. Bake 5 to 6 minutes.

For smooth scheduling, prepare dough and cut out paper patterns one day; refrigerate dough overnight. Next day, cut out and bake cookie pieces; decorate and assemble—or leave the assembling for another day.

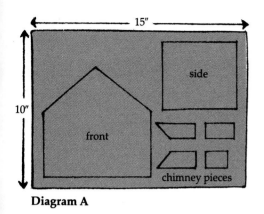

Diagram A

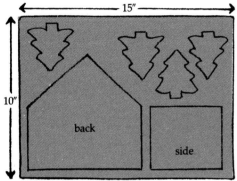

Diagram B

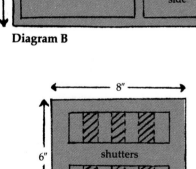

Diagram C
Remove every other strip.

side

chimney pieces

(cut 2)

chimney pieces

tree
(cut 4 or more)

roof
(cut 2)

front and back
(cut 2)

side
(cut 2)

PATTERN PLAN   Each square equals 1 inch.
A 3-inch tree-shaped cookie cutter can be used instead of pattern.

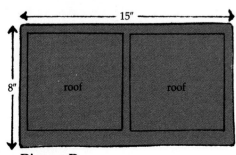

Diagram D

Details for front of chalet. Repeat window treatment on sides
and back; repeat attic trim on back if desired.

Trimming and Construction

1. Flatten 8 small red gumdrops and 8 small green gumdrops with rolling pin between 2 sheets of waxed paper. Cut 16 heart designs from red gumdrops with sharp knife or scissors. (Dip knife or scissors into hot water for easier cutting.) Cut accent designs from green gumdrops.

2. Prepare 1 package (7.2 ounces) fluffy white frosting mix as directed on package. Stir in 3 cups powdered sugar, ½ cup at a time, until thick and smooth. Keep covered.

3. Tint about ½ cup frosting with yellow food color. Frost door area and shutters using small spatula. Press gumdrop appliqués into position on shutters.

4. Place about ⅓ cup frosting in decorators' tube with #3 tip or use an envelope cone (page 7). Pipe lattice design for window panes on sides of house. Spread a strip of frosting on back of each shutter; press into position around panes.

5. Mix remaining frosting and ¼ cup cocoa. Keep covered. If frosting becomes too thick, stir in a few drops of water. Attach 9-inch strips to top and bottom of front and back of house, using cocoa frosting for "cement." Cut strips to fit along bottom of each side of house and below eaves if desired; attach with cocoa frosting. Cut strips for attic trim at a slant with sharp knife; cut strips for door trim. Attach with cocoa frosting.

6. Place remaining cocoa frosting in decorators' tube with #10 tip. Pipe strip above and below window lattice. Pipe ½-inch strip of frosting on inside vertical edges of back of house. Using a tray for the base, place back of house in vertical position on tray; press side pieces of house into frosting, making sure corners are square. Pipe cocoa frosting on inside vertical edges of front of house; press to front sides of house. Pipe frosting along inside vertical seam lines for reinforcement. Let set about 30 minutes. (Objects such as cans or bottles can be used to hold in place until frosting sets.)

7. Pipe frosting generously along top edges of front and back of house. Place roof pieces on top, making sure peaks meet in center.

8. Pipe frosting on inside vertical edges of 2 slanted chimney pieces. Press side pieces of chimney into frosting to form "box." Hold a few minutes until set; let dry. Pipe frosting on bottom edges of chimney; place on roof. Pipe any remaining frosting into seams as needed for reinforcement.

9. Arrange trees and path around house as desired. Sprinkle trees, path, house and tray lightly with powdered sugar.

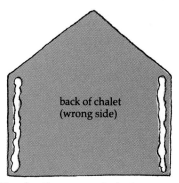

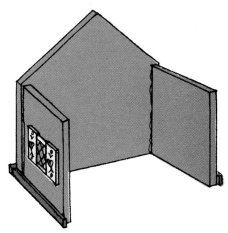

Pipe frosting on vertical edges on *inside* of back of chalet.

When pressing side pieces to frosting, make sure corners are square.

Pipe frosting on vertical edges on *inside* of front of chalet. Press front piece to sides.

Insert bottom slot of one tree into top slot of another; trees will stand upright.

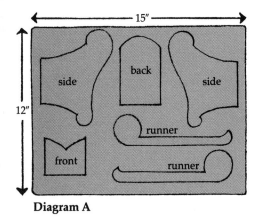

Diagram A

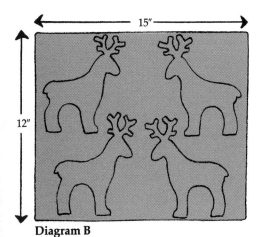

Diagram B

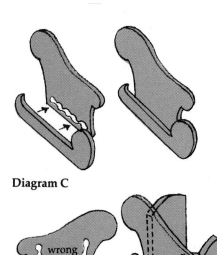

Diagram C

Diagram D

Christmas Sleigh and Reindeer

Preparation

1. Prepare Merry Christmas Molasses Cookie dough (page 7) as directed. Refrigerate at least 1 hour. Enlarge patterns according to scale (see Pattern Plan) and cut from heavy paper.

2. Divide dough into halves. Roll 1 half into rectangle, 15x12 inches, on lightly greased cookie sheet with floured stockinet-covered rolling pin. Heat oven to 375°. Place sleigh patterns on rectangle as shown in Diagram A. (The dough will expand during baking, so be sure to place the patterns at least ½ inch apart.) Cut around patterns with sharp knife; remove and reserve excess dough. Bake until no indentation remains when touched, 7 to 8 minutes. Cool 1 to 2 minutes; remove to wire rack.

3. Repeat Step 2 except place reindeer patterns on rectangle as shown in Diagram B. After removing excess dough, carefully insert part of wooden pick into each leg, leaving about ½ inch of pick exposed. (The picks will help support the reindeer.) Bake as directed.

4. Press remaining dough and the reserved dough into a ball. Roll into rectangle, 15x9 inches, on lightly greased cookie sheet. Trim evenly into rectangle, 14x8 inches. (This forms the base for the sleigh and reindeer.) Bake until no indentation remains when touched, 8 to 9 minutes. Cool 1 to 2 minutes; remove to wire rack.

Trimming and Construction

1. Prepare 1 package (7.2 ounces) fluffy white frosting mix as directed on package. Stir in 3 cups powdered sugar, ½ cup at a time, until thick and smooth. Measure and reserve 1 cup frosting; keep covered. Spread remaining frosting on baked rectangle base. (If a fluffier look is desired, prepare another package of frosting mix as directed above and spread on frosted base.)

2. Divide reserved frosting into 3 parts. Tint 1 part with green and 1 part with red food color. (Paste food color will make more vivid colors.)

3. Attach runners to sleigh with small amount of red frosting as shown in Diagram C. Place remaining red frosting in decorators' tube with #3 tip or use envelope cone (page 7); decorate sides of sleigh and reindeer as desired. Repeat with green and white frostings. Frost antlers with melted chocolate.

4. Pipe generous amount of remaining frosting on inside vertical edges of sleigh sides as shown in Diagram D. Holding one side of sleigh upright at one end of frosted base, press back of sleigh into frosting to join, then press front of sleigh into frosting. Press other side of sleigh against front and back pieces. Hold until secure. Pipe any remaining frosting along inside seams as needed for reinforcement. Place reindeer in front of sleigh, lightly pressing exposed portions of wooden picks into frosted base. Fill sleigh with pine sprigs, small toy Santa, cookies or small packages.

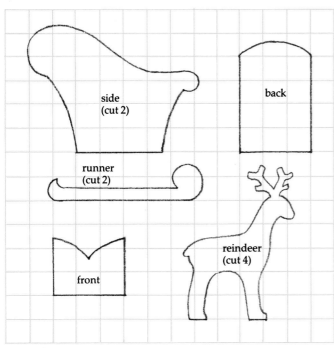

side
(cut 2)

back

runner
(cut 2)

front

reindeer
(cut 4)

PATTERN PLAN   Each square equals 1 inch.

Insert exposed portions of wooden picks into frosted base to hold reindeer upright.

Salt Dough Decorations

One of our favorite Christmas recipes has nothing to do with food. For that matter, you can't even eat it. But you can make very special holiday gifts from it—everything from Christmas tree ornaments to table accessories to gift tags. What is it? It's salt dough. Start off with the designs on the following pages (all developed exclusively for this book), then strike off on your own if you like. A word of warning: You'll be tempted to keep most of these presents for yourself.

Salt Dough

There's no need to make all the ornaments at one time. Wrap any extra dough in plastic wrap or aluminum foil and refrigerate; use within 2 weeks.

2 cups all-purpose flour	½ teaspoon powdered alum
1 cup salt	¾ cup water

Mix all ingredients completely with hands. (If dough is too dry, work in 1 to 1½ teaspoons water.) Form shapes as desired. Mark all details (facial features, clothing and the like) on surface of dough with wooden pick or sharp knife before baking.

To Roll: Roll dough ⅛ inch thick on lightly floured board. Cut with cookie cutters or cut around paper patterns with sharp knife.

To Mold by Hand: Form dough into shapes (flowers, fruits, animals, storybook characters) no more than ½ inch thick.

To Hang Ornaments: Cut fine craft wire 1½ to 2 inches long and twist several times to form loop; spread ends apart slightly and insert into unbaked ornament so that only loop shows. Or make a hole ¼ inch from top of ornament with end of plastic straw.

Heat oven to 250°. Place ornaments on ungreased cookie sheet. Bake until completely hard and dry, about 2 hours. Remove from cookie sheet; cool.

When cool, rub any rough edges with fine sandpaper until smooth. If desired, outline designs or other details to be painted with pencil. Paint with plastic-based poster or acrylic paint. Allow paint to dry. Place ornaments on waxed paper and seal by spraying with clear plastic (polyurethane) or brushing with clear shellac.   *About 5 dozen 2½-inch ornaments.*

Techniques and Tips

● Use only part of the dough at a time; keep remaining dough covered.

● Complete ornaments one at a time — don't use the assembly-line principle. If the surface of the basic shape dries out, if will be difficult to work with.

● If desired, dough can be tinted by dividing into several parts and kneading a different food color into each part. (Paste food color is more vivid.) After baking, seal as directed for painted ornaments.

● Indications for clothing, features and texture can be marked with a sharp knife or wooden pick. The wooden pick is best for small details.

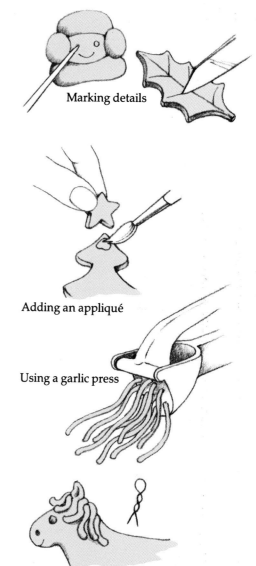

Marking details

Adding an appliqué

Using a garlic press

● Small appliqués add a nice touch: a star on a Christmas tree, a heart on a teddy bear, holly on a place card (see photograph on page 186). Roll a small portion of dough very thin (about ¹⁄₁₆ inch thick). Cut out all appliqués at one time using small canapé cutters or sharp knife. Put a dab of water on ornament where appliqué is desired, then top with appliqué. Baking will "cement" the appliqué in place.

● When adding small molded pieces (arms, legs, hats) to a three-dimensional ornament, always put a dab of water in the spot where the piece is going to be added. As with appliqués, baking will "cement" the piece in place.

● When cutting dough around a paper pattern, use a sharp knife.

● To make tiny ropes of dough for curls or texture, put dough through a garlic press. Work on a lightly floured surface to keep the tiny ropes from sticking.

● Form larger ropes of dough by hand-rolling.

● If making a complicated ornament, work right on the cookie sheet to minimize handling.

● If using a craft-wire loop to hang ornament, be sure to spread the ends before inserting in the ornament. This adds support.

● Small hairpins can also be used to hang ornaments. Spread ends apart and insert in ornament.

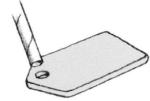

A craft-wire loop for hanging

● If using a plastic straw to make a hole for hanging, be sure the hole is at least ¼ inch from any edge.

● After baking, smooth any rough edges with fine sandpaper. An emery board will also do the trick.

● Remember to paint the sides and backs of ornaments.

● When adding painted accents, be sure the base color is dry.

● Giving an ornament as a Christmas present? It's a nice touch to add your name or initials and the year on the back.

● Larger ornaments can be hung on doors, in windows or in the center of a wreath. They make nice holiday paperweights too.

Making a hole with straw

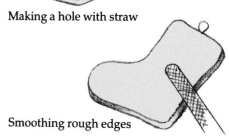

Smoothing rough edges

ANGEL'S HEAD

1. Roll dough ¼ to ³⁄₁₆ inch thick and cut out double wing shape with sharp knife, or form shape by hand.
2. Cut out or form head and shoulders; press gently onto wings.
3. Form small rope of dough and fit behind head for halo. Put dough through garlic press or hand-roll small pieces to form curls.

4. Form 2 flat circles and press lightly onto face for cheeks. Make indentations for mouth and eyes; notch wings with sharp knife.
5. Insert wire loop or make hole for hanging.
6. Bake as directed on page 178. Paint as desired. Let dry and seal.

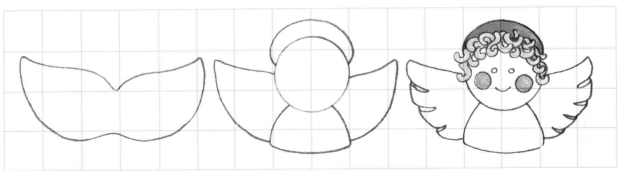

Each square equals ½ inch.

SNOWMAN

1. Roll dough ⅛ inch thick. Cut out basic shape with sharp knife.
2. Form hat brim and arms. Use piece of wooden pick for broom handle.
3. Overlap 2 pieces of dough for scarf.
4. Form broom and attach to handle. Make indentations for broom straws.

5. Insert wire loop or make hole for hanging.
6. Mold dough around piece of wooden pick for nose. Use small pieces of dough to form eyes or paint on after baking.
7. Bake as directed on page 178. Paint as desired. Let dry and seal.

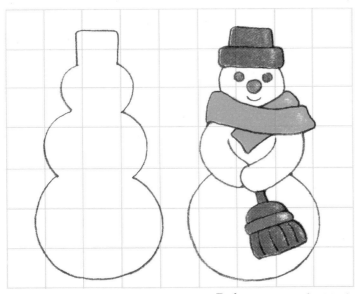

Each square equals ½ inch.

SANTA IN SLEIGH

1. Form dough into basic shape of sleigh, about ¼ inch thick.
2. Form runner and attach with 2 small "legs" of dough. Form body and 1 arm as a unit; attach to top of sleigh.
3. Form a ball and flatten for head. Form other arm and hat. Form a small ball for pompon.
4. Insert wire loop or make hole for hanging.
5. Form band for hat. Use a small ball of dough for nose. Mark details for mustache and mouth. Form beard.
6. Bake as directed on page 178. Paint as desired. Let dry and seal.

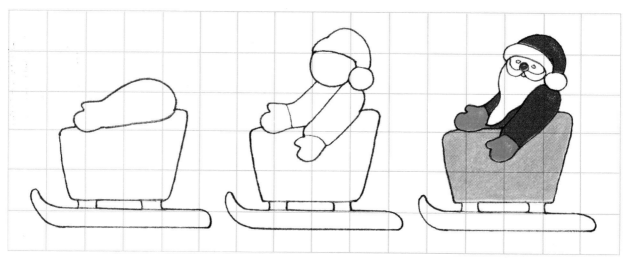

Each square equals ½ inch.

MOUSE WITH CANDLE

1. Form dough into body shape, about ¼ inch thick.
2. Form head and attach to body. Form arm and candle. Hand-roll a piece of dough for tail.
3. Form hat and place on head. Use a small ball of dough for pompon. Form collar.
4. Insert wire loop or make hole for hanging.
5. Form a small ball of dough and flatten for ear. Form a smaller ball and flatten for inside of ear. Use a small piece of dough for eye.
6. Bake as directed on page 178. Paint as desired (don't forget the whiskers). Let dry and seal.

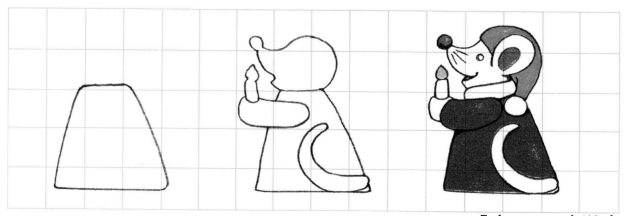

Each square equals ½ inch.

TEDDY BEAR

1. Form dough into 1-inch ball for body of bear; flatten one side slightly for back. Form a smaller ball for head.

2. Form 4 small rolls, each about ⅜ inch long, for arms and legs; taper one end of each roll and press onto body.

3. Form 3 small balls of dough; press onto head for ears and snout.

4. Form a tiny heart; press onto chest.

5. Insert wire loop or make hole for hanging.

6. Bake as directed on page 178. Paint as desired. Let dry and seal.

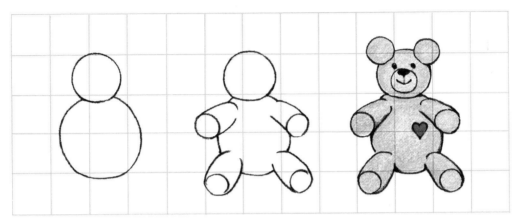

Each square equals ½ inch.

FILLED STOCKING

1. Roll dough ¼ inch thick and cut out stocking shape, or form shape by hand.

2. Form 2 small ropes of dough, 1½ inches long and ⅛ inch in diameter; twist together to form candy cane. Press one end of candy cane to back of stocking; curve other end over top of stocking.

3. Form head and shoulders of bear; press together. Press base of shoulders against back of stocking.

4. Flatten 3 small balls of dough slightly and press onto head for ears and snout. Form 2 small rolls for arms; taper one end of each roll and press onto shoulders. Mark details for cuff, toe and heel.

5. Insert wire loop or make hole for hanging.

6. Bake as directed on page 178. Paint as desired. Let dry and seal.

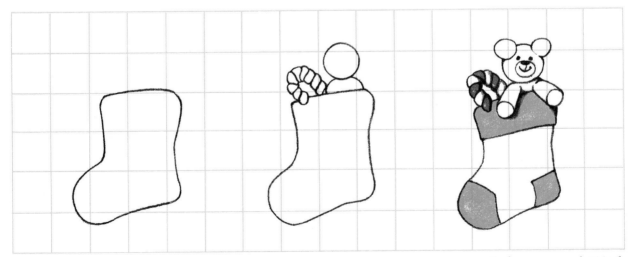

Each square equals ½ inch.

BOY AND GIRL SKATERS

1. Roll dough ⅛ inch thick. Cut out body shapes with sharp knife.
2. Form 2 small balls of dough and flatten for heads. Form arms, mittens and muff. Mark details for cuffs, sweater band, skirt and skate tops.
3. Form hats, earmuffs and scarves.

4. Insert wire loops or make holes for hanging.
5. Bend one end of 4 small paper clips and insert into boots to make skate blades.
6. Bake as directed on page 178. Paint as desired. Let dry and seal.

Each square equals ½ inch.

ROCKING HORSE

1. Roll dough ⅛ inch thick. Cut out basic shape with sharp knife.
2. Form saddle and place on horse. Add strap. Form tail.
3. Insert wire loop or make hole for hanging.

4. Hand-roll small pieces of dough or put through garlic press for mane; use 1 piece to shape stirrup. Use small pieces of dough to form eye and nostril.
5. Bake as directed on page 178. Paint as desired. Let dry and seal.

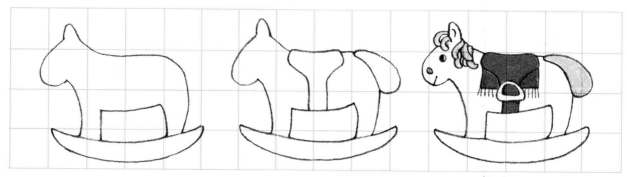

Each square equals ½ inch.

SANTA'S HEAD

1. Form dough into oval shape, about ¼ inch thick, for head. Hand-roll dough into rope, about ¼ inch in diameter and long enough to fit around oval (this will provide the base for Santa's beard). Wrap rope around oval and join.
2. Form hat and place on head. Form hat band. Use a small ball of dough for pompon.
3. Form a small ball for nose and place on face. Mark details for eyes. Form 2 flat circles and press lightly onto face for cheeks.

4. Hand-roll small ropes of dough and arrange one by one to form beard and mustache. Use shorter ropes to overlap mustache onto beard.
5. Insert wire loop or make hole for hanging.
6. Bake as directed on page 178. Paint as desired. Let dry and seal.
Note: To make a Christmas Elf, follow directions for Santa's Head except — make the head narrower, make the hat pointed and form a long nose.

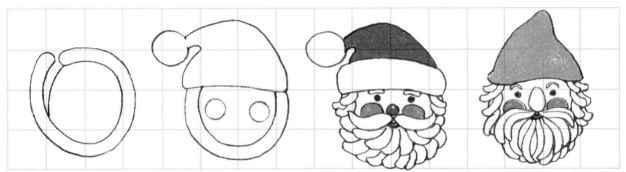

Each square equals ½ inch.

BRAIDED WREATH ORNAMENT

1. Hand-roll small pieces of dough into 3 ropes, each about 6 inches long and ¼ inch in diameter.
2. Moisten one end of each rope and pinch together; braid loosely. Moisten remaining ends; pinch to seal braid.
3. Moisten ends of braid and carefully curve to form wreath; pinch to seal.

4. Insert wire loop for hanging.
5. Decorate with holly leaves and berries or bow cut or formed from dough.
6. Bake as directed on page 178. Paint as desired. Let dry and seal.

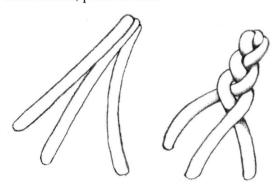

BRAIDED WREATH CANDLE HOLDERS

1. Follow Steps 1 and 2 as directed for Braided Wreath Ornament (page 185).
2. Turn braid on side; shape into ring around candle and press lightly to flatten; remove candle.

3. Decorate with holly leaves and berries or other shapes cut or formed from dough.
4. Bake as directed on page 178. Paint as desired. Let dry and seal.

BRAIDED WREATH NAPKIN RINGS

1. Cut strips, about 2½ inches wide and 4 inches long, from bottom of aluminum foil pie pan or cake pan. Shape each strip into a ring; staple ends together to form "mold."
2. Follow Steps 1 and 2 as directed for Braided Wreath Ornament (page 185).

3. Moisten ends of braid and shape around "mold," pinching ends together on top. Decorate with holly leaves and berries or other shapes cut or formed from dough.
4. Bake as directed on page 178. Remove molds. Paint as desired. Let dry and seal.

PLACE CARDS

1. Roll dough ¼ inch thick. Cut into rectangles, 2¼x1½ inches.
2. Cut triangles from dough to make stands. Make slightly shorter than height of place card and taper to form an angle less than 90°.

3. If using appliqués, cut and place on front of place card before baking.
4. Bake as directed on page 178. Attach triangle to back of place card with craft glue. Paint on names and decorations. Let dry and seal.

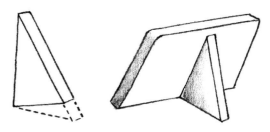

GIFT TAGS

1. Roll dough ⅛ to ³⁄₁₆ inch thick. Cut into tag shapes, about 2x1 inch.
2. If using appliqués, cut and place on front of tag before baking.

3. Make holes large enough for string or ribbon to go through.
4. Bake as directed on page 178. Paint on names and decorations. Let dry and seal.

DELLA ROBBIA WREATH CANDLE HOLDER

1. Hand-roll dough into rope, about ½ inch in diameter. Shape into ring around candle on cookie sheet, leaving ½ inch between candle and dough ring. Remove candle and flatten dough ring slightly to form base.
2. Roll dough ⅛ inch thick and cut out small leaf shapes with sharp knife. Moisten base with water; add leaves, overlapping and curving them to cover base completely.

3. Mold small fruit shapes (peaches, plums, apples, grapes, pears) from dough. Make creases in leaves and peaches and indentations for stems with wooden pick. Moisten bottoms of fruits with water; press onto leaf base.
4. Bake as directed on page 178. Paint realistically. Let dry and seal.
Note: For another design motif, cover base with holly leaves and berries.

Index